ARTIST and COMPUTER

ARTIST and COMPUTER

A CREATIVE COMPUTING Book

Creative Computing produces and distributes a wide variety of books, magazines, computer art prints, and other products related to computer applications in schools and homes. Available from Creative Computing are a complete catalog (25¢), a sample copy of *Creative Computing* Magazine ($1.50), or a subscription (see page 121). Creative Computing, P.O. Box 789-M, Morristown, NJ 07960, USA.

Additional copies of *Artist and Computer* are also available directly from the publisher, Harmony Books, a division of Crown Publishers, Inc., One Park Avenue, New York, NY 10016.

PRODUCED BY

Creative Computing Press
P.O. Box 789-M
Morristown, NJ 07960

PUBLISHED BY

Harmony Books
a division of
Crown Publishers, Inc.
One Park Avenue
New York, NY 10016

ARTIST AND COMPUTER

**Edited by
RUTH LEAVITT**

Creative Computing Press
Morristown, New Jersey

Harmony Books
New York, New York

Published simultaneously in Canada by General Publishing Company
Limited.
Printed in the United States of America.

Library of Congress Catalog Card Number: 76-440

Library of Congress Cataloging in Publication Data
Main entry under title:
Artist and computer.
1. Computer art. 2. Art, Modern—20th century.
I. Leavitt, Ruth.
N7433.8.A77 1975 702'.8'54 76-440
ISBN 0-517-52787-1
ISBN 0-517-52735-9 pbk.

Creative Computing Press
Morristown, New Jersey

First Printing, June, 1976.

To Jay and Danny

CONTRIBUTORS

Charles and Colette Bangert
729 Illinois Street
Lawrence, Kansas 66044

Mánuel Barbadillo
Parque de Torremolinos, 9
Torremolinos (Malaya)
Spain

Vicky Meyer Chaet
228 Kipling
Palo Alto, California 94306

Charles Csuri
Art Dept./146 Hopkins Hall
Ohio State University
128 North Oval Drive
Columbus, Ohio 43210

Herbert W. Franke
D-8195 Puppling 40
Pupplinger Au, near Munich
Fed. Rep. Germany

Aldo Giorgini
School of Civil Engineering
Purdue University
West Lafayette, Indiana 47907

Miljenenko Horvat
3452 Henri-Julien
Montreal, Canada

Karen Huff
Computing Center
Kansas State University
Manhattan, Kansas 66506

Edward Ihnatowicz
Mechanical Engr. Dept.
University College - Gower Street
London, England WC1E 6BT

Hiroshi Kawano
3-16-1-15, Aoto
Katsushika-Ku
Tokyo, Japan

Kenneth Knowlton
810 Belvidere Avenue
Plainfield, New Jersey 07062

William Kolomyjec
Engr. Insts. Serv. Dept.
College of Engineering
Michigan State University
East Lansing, Michigan 48824

Ben Laposky
301 S. 6th Street
Cherokee, Iowa 51012

Ruth Leavitt
5315 Dupont Avenue, South
Minneapolis, Minnesota 55419

Kurt Lauckner
Math Dept.
Eastern Michigan University
Ypsilanti, Michigan 48197

Tony Longson
Dept. of Computer Science
Hatfield Polytechnic
P.O. Box 109
Hatfield, Herts. England

Robert Mallary
Art Dept.
University of Massachusetts
Amherst, Massachusetts 01002

Edward Manning
972 East Broadway
Stratford, Connecticut 06497

Aaron Marcus
Dept. of Architecture and Urban Planning
Princeton University
Princeton, New Jersey 08540

Leslie Mezei
Dept. of Computer Science
University of Toronto
Toronto, Canada M5S 1A4

Manfred Mohr
58 Bld. Latour-Maubourg
Paris - 7, France

Vera Molnar
54, rue Halle
Paris 14E, France

Ann Murray
Watson Gallery
Wheaton College
Norton, Massachusetts 02766

Jacques Palumbo
c/o Gilles Gheerbrant Galerie
2130 Crescent
Montreal H3G 2B8
Canada

Duane M. Palyka
Computer Science - Merrill Engr. Bld.
The University of Utah
Salt Lake City, Utah 84112

Larry Press
128 Park Place
Venice, California 90291

Joseph Scala
Dept. of Visual & Performing Arts
University Avenue
Syracuse University
Syracuse, New York 13210

Patsy Scala
960 Westcott Street
Syracuse, New York 13210

Lillian Schwartz
524 Ridge Road
Watchung, New Jersey 07060

Peter Struycken
Prinsengracht 825
Amsterdam, Holland

Synthavision/Larry Elin
3 Westchester Plaza
Elmsford, New York 10523

Christopher William Tyler
Smith-Kettlewell Institute
2232 Webster Street
San Francisco, California 94115

Roger Vilder
410 Avenue Champagneur
Montreal, Quebec 3P5
Canada

John Whitney
600 Erskin Drive
Pacific Palisades, California 90272

Edward Zajec
via D. Chiesa 18
Trieste, Italy

PREFACE

The relationship between artist and computer is important both to people in the arts and sciences and to society as a whole. (The union of art and science in computer art is reflective of the times in which we live.) Ours is a technological society, one which demands inter-disciplinary approaches to problems. Our lives are closely linked to one another. Therefore, we must communicate.

Assumptions about computer art are varied. They range from the naive belief that computers will take the place of human artists to the more sophisticated belief that soon the Leonardo of computer art will come. This person would be scientist, programmer, humanist, and artist—the true universal person. Computer art challenges our traditional beliefs about art: how art is made, who makes it, and what is the role of the artist in society.

The general public, and the artist in particular, have been conditioned to react negatively to computers. The uninitiated artist asks: what can this machine do for me? Really, the question should be: what can I do with this machine? The computer can function for the artist at many different levels. The artist has only to choose what role he/she wishes the computer to play. Apart from producing finished pieces of artwork, as William Kolomyjec does, one may simply allow the computer to function as an idea machine. This is evidenced in several articles. Karen Huff, for example, describes how the computer is used to visualize fabric before it is actually woven. As opposed to weaving on graph paper by hand, the computer removes the automatic color preference found in that traditional method. Moreover, by studying computer illustrations the softening of contours, which was seen only after a weaving was removed from the loom, can now be predicted.

Another artist, Robert Mallary, describes how he uses the machine to create new artforms by means of new programs. He creates sculpture with his program Tran 2 and graphics with GRAF/D and TRPL. A 3-dimensional program called SHAPE 3/D is used as a tool in research of aesthetics and art theory. Moreover, he is involved in using the computer to simulate and make decisions on land use and design. Another approach is found in the route Joseph Scala describes. He is experimenting and creating works of art with programs that already exist.

There are vast areas and levels of exploration available to the artist. The computer helps the artist to perceive in a new way. Its features blend with those of its user to form a new type of art. The combination of artist and oil paint is, for example, a different statement than that same artist and watercolors. The medium changes the statement. The artist now goes to an art supply store to purchase a given set of tools, whereas the computer artist can create the tools he will use. This is remarkable and allows for unlimited possibilities in the art to be created. Every program functions as a new set of tools. The type and quality of work produced on the computer depend both on the artist who uses the machine and the program.

Works produced on the computer do not have a unique style. It is difficult, at best, to identify a piece of art as having been created with the aid of a computer. Many of these styles existed independently of the computer. Perhaps if the machine had been available at the inception of these styles, they would have been explored more thoroughly. I found it very amusing to read in the exhibition catalogue 'PAINTING: NEW OPTIONS' at Walker Art Center, Minneapolis, Minnesota, 1972:

Jennifer Bartlett's first gridworks were series of numbers drawn on graph paper, that indispensable work surface of the conceptual artist of the 1960s. She found that by substituting colored dots for the numbers, she could transform her mathematical sequences into visually independent forms. The enameled steel plates of her present work, elegantly custom-made to the artist's specifications, have gridworks of 2304 tiny squares within which the artist paints her pointillist dot patterns. Installed on a wall in rows, these modular plates become miniature panel paintings that explore variations on certain mathematical-graphic themes. Some rows establish an almost cinematic narrative of visual events; others form continuous patterns that, at a distance, have a brilliant optical effect. Though Bartlett consciously avoids painterly processes, her art is a mixture of visual improvisation and preconceived formulae. A plate often begins with an arbitrary unit, such as the continuous black border, or a single random dot; a quasi-mathematical system dictates the rest, and in the modular works this same system carries over from plate to plate. In SERIES VIII, a 36-plate work, the first plate's design was generated by an isolated white dot, followed by white and yellow, followed by white, yellow, and red, and so forth. The second plate retains this formula for color sequence, but begins with a yellow dot. The parabola pattern that appears on each plate of the set is not the product of a mathematical equation [Bartlett does not work with computer-produced graphics] but is the result of the additive dot-by-dot system she selects.

The explanation of her work only made me think how inappropriate it was not to have used a computer. Furthermore, in the same catalogue we find an example of modular art in Sol LeWitt's wall drawings. His work parallels that of Barbadillo. Modular art is an approach often used in computer art. However, in this case no mention is made of computers. It is obvious that people at Walker Art Center have a stereotype image of computer art. Actually, there is no such thing as 'computer art'!

Different artists use the machine in different ways to produce different types of art. Edward Ihnatowicz is deeply interested in artificial intelligence and uses this approach in creating cybernetic sculpture. Aaron Marcus' work shows his interest in concrete poetry. He creates picture environments and his poem drawings give new meaning and depth to words. Duane Palyka uses a color television monitor attached to a computer system and paints pictures in an unprecedented manner. The Bangerts' drawings appear hand-made. Aldo Giorgini's moire patterns have the look of optical art. Each takes advantage of different features offered by the computer.

I have been lecturing to groups of adults and students in the last few years, both on my own work and on computer art in general. These groups have included students of art, art history, computer science, futuristics, etc. I found that irrespective of background, questions concerning motivation were repeatedly asked. I had been thinking about the answers to these questions for some time. When Dave Ahl asked me to put together a special edition of *Creative Computing* magazine devoted to computer art, I felt that this would be an ideal opportunity to discover how other computer artists would respond to these questions. I was curious to see if they shared my feelings. Since previous books on computer art had only documented the state of the art, I felt that now it would be interesting to have the artists discuss their art with regard to these questions:

- *How/why did you become involved with the computer (in producing art)?*
- *What is your art background?*
- *What role does the computer play for you ... simulation, tool, etc.? What is your role?*
- *Are your computer works related to non-computer art?*
- *Do you have a final image in mind when work begins?*
- *Could your work be done without the aid of a computer? If yes, why use the computer?*
- *To what extent are you involved in the technical production of your work, for example, in programming?*
- *Do you feel art work created with a computer has now or will have an impact on art as a whole in the future?*
- *Do you intend to continue using the computer to create art pieces?*
- *Do you recommend the use of the computer for others in creating works of art?*

Some of the authors address the questions in their articles; some do not. Many of the papers are purely statements about the artist's work. Just as the artists' artwork differs, so do their papers. It is important for artists to be able to discuss their work in their own words. Therefore, the papers in this book are presented with a minimum of editing.

I am grateful to all who submitted manuscripts for this book. Each contribution helps clarify the relationship between artist and computer.

Ruth Leavitt
Minneapolis, Minnesota
February 1976

CONTENTS

ANN H. MURRAY

The idea of organizing a Computer Graphics Show at Wheaton College in the spring of 1975 first came to me when I read an article on Norton Starr's work. Norton teaches mathematics at Amherst College, where my husband was then teaching geology. I had several discussions with him, and he was able to make numerous suggestions on important people in the field of Computer Art. He also demonstrated the use of the computer to generate and execute a design. I began to do a lot of reading on the subject, and eventually put together the show. Initially I had intended for it to focus on work being produced in New England (to help control transportation costs) but the exhibition eventually grew to include work from throughout the country. In my catalogue introduction I wanted to avoid a lengthy description of computer techniques, because I felt that these had been covered in other publications, and from a far more technical view than I, as an art historian, was able to present. Rather I had become aware during my graduate student years that mathematics had always played a very important role in works of art—certainly not in every painting or sculpture, but in a number of significant ones, especially during the late 19th and early 20th centuries. So in the catalogue I aimed to discuss computer graphics not as the products of complex machines unique to the modern age, but as related to a long standing interest in, and preoccupation with science and mathematics on the part of artists—particularly artists who sought to create visual images based upon some sort of universally valid order.

The following is my introduction to that catalogue.

Computer Graphics in Historical Perspective

Several years ago Robert L. Herbert introduced his well-known essay on Neo-Impressionism with the following anecdote:

> At an exhibition of Neo-Impressionism in 1893, a woman peered over the entrance turnstile at the paintings inside, while debating whether or not to pay the modest fee to one of the painters seated at the cash box. 'Were these done by machine, Monsieur?' she asked. 'No, Madame,' he calmly replied, 'they were done by hand.'[1]

The woman's confusion, amusing as it may be, was not without foundation. For Georges Seurat, chief innovator of the new style, had transformed the loosely applied brushstrokes and intuitively broken colors of Impressionism into a fabric of tiny, uniform, color-bearing dots which he repeated over the surface of the canvas with machine-like regularity. By dividing his colors in this calculated manner, he attempted to apply in painting the optical laws described in modern scientific studies of color such as Ogden Rood's *Modern Chromatics* (French ed., 1881) and M.E. Chevreul's *De la loi du contraste simultané des couleurs* (1839).

Other scientific principles also intrigued Seurat. He followed the latest experiments being conducted on mental patients to determine the psychological effects of linear movement and of color, and he attempted to apply the results of these studies in his paintings in an effort to evoke a particular mood in the viewer. His attempt to elucidate a permanent structure underlying the ephemeral surface appearances which so delighted the Impressionists, occasionally led Seurat to construct the composition of a painting or a drawing according to the mathematical ratios which defined the ideal proportions of the golden section. All of this was in pursuit of an allusive 'scientific esthetique' described by his friend Charles Henry (1859-1926), who lectured and published prolifically on mathematics, psychology and aesthetics.

The emergence of the first digital computers in the early 1940's opened up the possibility of pursuing a scientific aesthetic along lines more appropriate for an era of space-age technology. This, of course, did not happen overnight, and the computer remains, to a great extent, a scientific tool rather than an artistic medium. Yet by the mid-sixties the boundaries had become less clearly defined. Occasional investigators who had begun by using the computer to obtain information in the form of plotted diagrams quickly realized that their 'scientific pictures' often had considerable aesthetic merit in their own right.[2] Before long a number of mathematicians and engineers had begun to explore these aesthetic possibilities apart from any scientific objectives. Drawings produced with the aid of the computer made their way into fashionable New York galleries, and 1968 saw the first major international exhibition of computer art, 'Cybernetic Serendipity,' held at the Institute of Contemporary Arts in London.

At the present time the computer is being utilized by graphic designers, printmakers, sculptors, film makers, architects and choreographers. Many prefer to work in conjunction with a programmer who can translate their ideas into the mathematical language of the machine. Others have learned to program their ideas directly, thereby maintaining an immediate involvement with their medium as has been the case in more traditional forms of art.

The creation of a two-dimensional computer-generated design requires a number of steps.[3] First the artist must state his idea in terms of a program, which is typed onto punch cards and fed into the computer. On the basis of these instructions (known as 'software') the machine (or 'hardware') computes the coordinates of the desired points. It is possible for the artist to program random as well as ordered elements into his prospective design, and to combine them in whatever proportions seem aesthetically effective. The range of possible effects extends from abstract geometric patterns to illusionistic landscapes.

In the more sophisticated systems a visual image first materializes when a beam of electrons connects the points by a series of straight lines which it successively 'draws' on the screen of a cathode ray tube (CRT). At this stage of its realization, the picture appears as a white pattern on a dark ground, and looks as if it were being viewed on an ordinary television set. This provides the artist with an opportunity to correct errors or to otherwise modify his design before recording it on film or reproducing it in graphic form. When satisfied with the visual effect as it appears on the screen the artist may choose to have it photographed by an interconnected camera, or alternatively, he may instruct the computer to have the picture mechanically plotted onto paper in black or colored inks. It is also possible to introduce color to a drawing via standard silkscreening techniques.

Computer-generated graphics have affinities both with the drawing and printmaking media. Like drawings executed by hand, the image is applied in ink directly onto paper. But unlike a traditional drawing, which is one of a kind, the computer picture can be reproduced any number of times by re-running the program and replotting the results. In this respect it is more closely related to a lithograph, in which the original image is drawn onto a lithographic stone and then multiplied by printing onto paper. It should, however, be pointed out that replotting a computer design does not insure an image identical to that in the initial drawing. The mechanical plotter can lose its orientation, thereby producing a strikingly different effect

which may have aesthetic merit in its own right. It is also possible for the pen to run dry temporarily, creating random patterns of linear activity versus void on the surface. In some instances these too can yield aesthetically pleasing results which the artist may choose to exploit.

If graphics, films and even three-dimensional sculpture created with the aid of computers seem like the epitome of a scientific aesthetic, it is precisely their mathematical predictability which often prevents computer-generated designs from being accepted as legitimate art. As A. Michael Noll has pointed out,[4] intuition has always been a valued component of the creative process, and there would seem to be little room for an intuitive response on the part of the mechanical plotter taking its orders from a program in which everything is specified in mathematical terms.

Yet the emergence of a medium which is totally dependent upon a mathematical foundation might be viewed as an extreme manifestation of the same interest in mathematics previously displayed by several important artists of the modern era. The challenge of restructuring nature upon a universally valid geometrical framework intrigued others besides Seurat. The ideal golden section also lurks beneath the formal complexities of Juan Gris's Cubist still-lifes, and in fact 'La Section d'Or' provided the

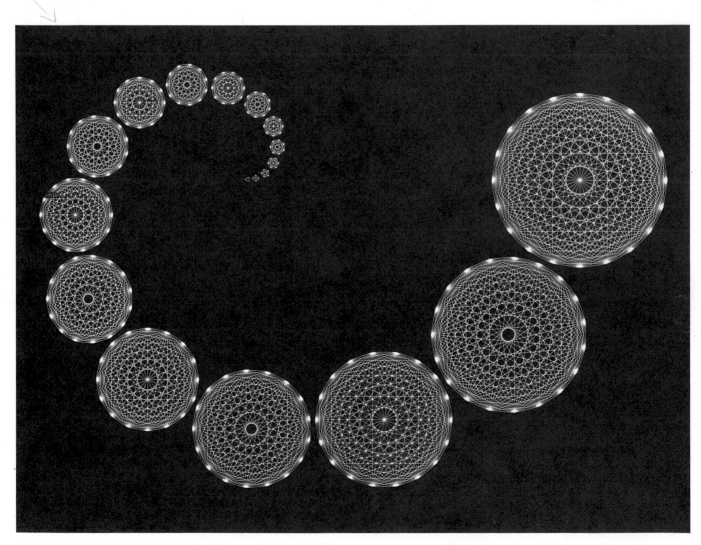

'Archimedean Spiral' by Norton Starr, 1973. The print is a photo reversal of a black ink drawing on white paper. It is in the Wheaton College collection, Norton, MA.

title for one of the most ambitious exhibitions of Cubist painting held in the years immediately preceding World War I. Roger Allard, who championed the Cubist style in a 1912 essay for the German almanac, Der Blaue Reiter (1912), maintained that a cubist painter experiences space in terms of mathematical equations and ratios, and seeks to elucidate their hidden rhythms.[5]

Wassily Kandinsky, the Russian leader of the Blaue Reiter group in Munich, was intrigued by the notion that beneath the structure of a painting lie hidden geometrical configurations which speak to the soul rather than to the eye. In his famous essay entitled Uber das Geistige in der Kunst (1912), Kandinsky suggested that the relationships among these configurations might even be expressed mathematically, although more in terms of 'irregular' than of 'regular' figures. He stated emphatically that "The final abstract expression of every art is number."[6] (Kandinsky's italics)

In another article written for Der Blaue Reiter Kandinsky discussed his views on the use of geometric forms and mathematical relationships as he felt they were being applied in Cubism. After commenting that the Cubists' use of the number is far too limited, he argued that widely divergent numbers such as 1 and 0.3333 are equally valid, equally vital inner-vibrating beings. "Why," he asked, "should one be satisfied with 1? Why should one exclude 0.3333?"[7] Kandinsky would, no doubt, have been disconcerted with the knowledge that one day such numbers could be programmed into a computer, and their 'inner significance' projected onto the face of a cathode ray tube. Nevertheless, the emergence of such a picture ironically fulfills a strange prediction by Kandinsky himself, who envisioned an art form which would radiate directly from the artist's mind without the aid of pigment or brushes.[8]

For many the computer seems not only to limit the artist's intuitive response to his own unfolding creation, but also prevents him from leaving any personal trace in the execution of the work. Granted he can devise a program uniquely suited to a particular artistic conception, and can accept, reject, or modify the image as it emerges on the screen. He can even vary the quality of line and introduce a variety of coloristic effects. Yet somehow all this seems limited when measured against an 'old master' drawing, in which every line and every nuance directly reflects its creator's individual response to the medium.

However, to consider computer-generated graphics in this light is to remove them from their proper artistic context. Like so many 'conceptual' works of the past several years, the creative process is centered not in the execution of the work, but in the artist's mind as he conceives the idea for a piece. In fact, it is often the all-important idea rather than the individual's technical mastery of a particular medium which constitutes the success of a painting or a sculpture. The realization of the artist's mental image can even occur without his physical involvement, or even his presence, as evidenced by reputable sculptors who send their specifications to the foundry (jokingly dubbed the 'sculpture factory') where the piece is executed. Viewed in this context the computer should be considered not as a gimmick but as a tool capable of freeing the artist from tasks which otherwise would prove tedious or even impossible to accomplish by hand.

In many respects the utilization of the computer for artistic endeavors parallels the emergence of photography as the 'mechanical medium' of the nineteenth century. In its early days many painters felt threatened by the camera's ability to reproduce a scene with greater verisimilitude than was possible by means of brushes and pigment. However, those painters confident enough of their own superiority over the machine quickly began to regard the camera as a valuable tool for recording the physical characteristics of a person, place or object in a form which could be consulted easily for future reference. It is not surprising that both Eugene Delacroix and Gustave Courbet occasionally worked from photographs rather than from live models, or that Paul Gauguin drew on photographs for the artifacts depicted in some of his Oceanic scenes. Only after the photograph was accepted at the level of an artistic aid could it ultimately cease to threaten painting and develop into a creative medium in its own right.

Much of the computer-generated graphic work to date must properly be considered as the groundwork for a similar type of development toward an autonomous artistic medium. The first decade of experimentation has shown that the computer can be programmed to simulate the styles of previously existing art. As one might expect, it is well suited to designs which are basically linear and geometric, but by using a special program initially developed by Ken Knowlton of the Bell Telephone Laboratories, it can also reproduce tonal gradations. Other programs allow it to execute original designs in an amazingly free-hand manner, or to draw complicated buildings and their landscape settings in perfect perspective. One senses, however, that the machine's potential as a tool for creating completely new forms of art has hardly been tapped, although its obvious value in the fields of architecture and commercial design has already been acknowledged, and it is currently being utilized in highly creative ways by respected filmmakers like Stan Vanderbeek, John Whitney and Lillian Schwartz. The value of the computer for artists lies not in its ability to mimic what man can do, but in providing a means for man to accomplish artistic endeavors which ordinarily would lie beyond his technical scope.

It is almost impossible to imagine what art lovers can expect from the computer in the future. In discussing its artistic consequences, A. Michael Noll has predicted the development of special 'programming languages' which could be geared to the requirements of any individual artist, and which would eventually become "as natural to use as the conventional brushes and oils."[9] If Noll is correct, and if more and more artists learn programming techniques in order to realize their ideas directly without the programmer as middleman, the concept of a bona-fide computer-based 'scientific aesthetic' may begin to seem less foreign.

Norton, Massachusetts
October 1975

FOOTNOTES

1. Robert L. Herbert, *Neo-Impressionism*, exh. cat. (New York: The Solomon R. Guggenheim Foundation, 1968), p. 14.
2. Herbert W. Franke, *Computer Graphics—Computer Art*, trans. Gustav Metzger (London: Phaidon, 1971), p. 59.
3. A. Michael Noll, "The Digital Computer as a Creative Medium," *IEEE Spectrum* (October 1967), p. 90.
4. *Ibid.*, pp. 89-90.
5. Roger Allard, "Die Kennzeichen der Erneuring in der Malerei," in *Der Blaue Reiter*, ed. Franz Marc and Wassily Kandinsky (Munich, 1912); new edition with documentary notes by Klaus Lankheit (Munich, 1965), pp. 77-86.
6. Wassily Kandinsky, *Über das Geistige in der Kunst* (Munich, 1912); English edition: *Concerning the Spiritual in Art*, trans. Ralph Manheim (New York, 1947), p. 73.
7. Wassily Kandinsky, "Über die Formfrage," in *Der Blaue Reiter*, p. 173.
8. Sixten Ringbom, "Art in the 'Epoch of the Great Spiritual': Occult Elements in the Early Theory of Abstract Painting," *J Warb*, 29 (1966) p. 416.
9. A. Michael Noll, "Computers and the Visual Arts," *Design and Planning 2*, ed. Martin Krampen and Peter Seitz (New York: Hastings House, Publishers, Inc. 1967), p. 79.

ROBERT MALLARY

"How/why did you become involved with the computer in producing art?"

My involvement with the computer is the consequence of a long-standing interest in art-and-technology that extends back to the very beginning of my career in 1936. My first enthusiasm was the Mexican school of mural painting and my model was David Alfaro Siqueiros, who as early as 1932 was advocating a revolution in the tech-nology of art. For Siqueiros this meant using the airbrush and synthetic automobile lacquers to paint his out-sized propaganda murals, and I began by following in his footsteps.

During the forties I was experimenting with both acrylic and polyester plastics, with fluorescent dyes and pigments, and spent a couple of months researching a cinematographic approach to kinetic sculpture based on what I described as 'multiplanar sequential image projection.' In 1951 I constructed an eight-bladed *stroboplane* to test the principle, and demonstrated the device in a one-man show in Los Angeles a year later. Along with some drawings on plaster I also displayed a cluster of transparent fluorescent sculptures illuminated by black light. These latter triggered my first publicity break—a full page color reproduction in *Time*.

I turned to the computer in 1967 on learning for the first time about its ability to generate and transform images. Almost immediately I realized that my earlier idea of multiplanar image synthesis could be used to describe three-dimensional forms within the computer by slicing and stacking them as two-dimensional shapes—something like a contour map. The result was my computer sculpture program TRAN2, the first version of which was written in 1968 for the IBM 1130 system at Amherst College.

"What is your art background?"

My reputation, such as it is, is based not so much on my activities in art-and-technology and with the computer as on the Neo-Dada and *assemblage* constructions I was doing in New York about 1960. However, even this 'junk art' could not have been made but for polyester resin, which I came across in 1946 as a consequence of my explorations in art-and-technology. But I gave up using all plastics, solvents and spray cans after 1962 on learning they were poisoning me, and for the five years before dis-

'Quad IV', laminated marble, 11 inches high. The computer sculpture program TRAN 2 was used to design the sculpture and draw the cross sections, which were transferred to the marble slabs and traced. The slabs were cut out, laminated together with epoxy, then ground to a smooth contour and polished.

covering the computer, had virtually no explicit involvement with art-and-technology.

The year 1967 was crucial for me in a number of other ways. It was the year I began teaching at the University of Massachusetts in Amherst and had the opportunity to try out computers, and it was also about that time that art-and-technology shook the art world—thanks mainly to Robert Rauchenberg and his friends in the Experiments in Art and Technology group (E.A.T.). Unfortunately, this high-octane group, after launching art-and-technology in this country, promptly sank it with a series of technically amateurish and Pop-ridden exhibitions that were not long in giving art-and-technology a bad name. Those of us who are really serious about art-and-technology (and have stuck with it during hard times) are still paying the price. But things are looking better. For since its nadir about 1971 the movement has been reviving. In fact, its prospects might even be called promising now that it has struck up an alliance with the computer and has achieved a solid base of operations in a few key colleges and universities.

However, the artists and engineers who organized E.A.T. should be given their due. Although they certainly did not invent art-and-technology out of whole cloth (whose roots are as diverse as Constructivism, the Bauhaus, and the Mexicans—to mention only a few), they nevertheless managed to contribute a catchy if less than euphonious name for a movement that had long been in need of one.

In sum, my art background is art-and-technology, and my enduring interest is the potential of science and technology for art.

"What role does the computer play for you?"

The power of the computer in art is that it can play a variety of roles, many of them cybernetic, or 'brain-like.' The computer, like any tool or machine, extends human capabilities. But it is unique in that it extends the power of the mind as well as the hand. Hence, a clear distinction must be made between this brain-like function and the output instrumentalities (like film, video, photography, holography, kinetic sculpture, graphics, light art, etc.) through which this power is expressed. This explains why the computer is not an art medium as such, and why the phrase 'computer art,' if used to convey this meaning, is a misnomer. Properly defined, the role of the computer is that of a key cybernetic component in a host medium, art form, or art-generating system where it performs a variety of functions, some of them far more sophisticated than others from a cybernetic standpoint. In other words, some of them have more to do with the brain than the hand, and in this respect are more portentous in their long-term implications for art. And it is these cybernetic implications that interest me the most.

For example, one artist might use the computer for its speed, precision, and implacable tirelessness; another for its ability to imitate biological, physiological, or psychological stimulus/response interactions; another for its ability to simulate other kinds of art; another as a way of mediating the flow of energy and information within a transductive system (as when sound ignites the visual kinetics on a CRT or video display); another for its ability to regulate precise and fast-moving performances (as in a kinetic laser system); another for its ability to calculate the minute 'iterations-with-a-difference' of a spiralgraphic-like composition; and another for its ability to calculate a hologram, or the small differences of imagery in a stereo pair.

As for myself, although the underlying concept of TRAN2 has yet to be fully implemented, eventually this sculpture program will exploit the computer's interactive 'conversational' capabilities to speed and enhance the design of sculptural forms, continuously shaping and reshaping them by means of a large library of transformation algorithms and routines. Another program of mine, called GRAF/D, uses the plotter for no better reason than to draw a grid of lines straighter, faster, and more evenly than I could by hand. Yet another program, called TRPL, uses the machine to calculate the interpolations between a set of master lines, while also incrementing and decrementing the intervals between the lines. In this case these

'2-color computer graphic', 9¾x9¾ inches, 1972.
A two-color plotter graphic made on the Amherst College IBM 1130 system. The program, called GRAF/D, was written in Fortran IV by the artist. The program stops while the pens are changed by hand. Felt tip and ball point pens are combined in the same drawing.

'3-Color Computer Graphic', 12¾ high x 9¾ inches wide, 1972.
A three-color graphic made on the Amherst College IBM system. The program, called GRAF/D, was written by the artist in Fortran IV. The program stops while the pens are changed by hand. Felt tip and ballpoint colored pens are combined in the same drawing.

microscopic nuances are beyond my ability either to calculate or to draw.

But within the context of the computer itself almost all of the capabilities I have just mentioned are somewhat on the order of mechanical skills when compared to the computer's truly cybernetic potential. This comes into play when the computer begins to make aesthetic distinctions, choices, and assessments, and when it has been programmed with the information needed for it to organize and compose art of a superior quality automatically and seemingly 'on its own.' Used this way, the computer can be turned into a marvelous tool for research in art theory and aesthetics, and for testing the structural syntax, principles, devices, and ratios against the quality of the serial output. Because the computer is preeminently a calculating machine it can output as alphanumeric listings the quantifiable features and relationships needed for close study and analysis.

SHAPE was written five years ago as a start in this direction, and last summer its name was changed to SHAPE3/D when it was enlarged as a 3-dimensional program for organizing a repertoire of solids into various kinds of compositions, some simple and some complex. Thirty parameters can define an enormous range of forms, features, and compositional set-ups which can be rotated for viewing from any arbitrary perspective. The ratios of size, spacing, height, color, empty-to-filled space, and other characteristics can all be prespecified within an approximate range, while using the random number subroutine to generate the 'variety-within-specified-limits' which is the essence of the approach.

Last summer an interdisciplinary group of artists, environmental planners, and computer specialists on our campus was funded by the National Endowment for the Arts to study the aesthetic aspect of stripmine reclama-

tion, approaching it from the standpoint of landscape design and large-scale environmental sculpture. This is very much a computer-oriented project in which we will be combining into a single integrated package a number of the computer capabilities just enumerated.

For example, using the system in its interactive mode, the designer/sculptor will compose landform arrangements based on a substructure of geometrical primitives, which at the right moment can be joined and unified by a curve-fitting algorithm that scans the topographical surface. Or, put into the automated mode, the computer will suggest ideas of its own—all of them in accord with a complex web of criteria that, in addition to the explicitly aesthetic specifications, also includes environmental, land use, cost, and other requirements that must be considered. These plans and designs will then be outputted in a variety of visual forms (film, video, stereo, CRT display, plotter, etc.) for the more efficient and vivid communication of this visual information. What I am describing, of course, is an *ultimate* objective. Our immediate goals are more modest.

In short, the 'role' of the computer for me is precisely its diversity of roles, most of them cybernetic in some way or degree.

"Are your computer works related to non-computer art?"

Definitely yes—particularly to the geometry and formalism of Constructivism and Neo-Plasticism. In fact, the more geometric and mathematically-based kinds of computer art (like spiralgraphics) might even qualify as a subset and off-shoot of Constructivism, which in turn is likely to be both revitalized and broadened by this new development in art-and-technology. And the same holds for Op Art, in which are buried a number of still unexplored potentials that only a computer can uncover. Although the moire patterns generated by my program TRPL are surely not Op Art as such, they suggest something of what I have in mind.

"Do you have a final image in mind when work begins?"

It is a common fallacy that artists simply copy a ready-made image that is fixed and unchanging in the mind's eye. The error here is in thinking of the creative process as essentially static and undialectical. The start-up stage for most artists is a rather vague idea that evolves towards definition and completeness in the course of the work itself (and in the case of Abstract Expressionism and gesture painting this open-ended strategy is practically a *sine-qua-non*). Moreover, contemporary artists are likely to jettison the original idea completely if something better happens along while the work is underway.

I can't see that the computer changes this very much. In developing, then using a program so as to express the original idea, there are usually experiments with the parameter settings to get the most out of the program and optimize the output. Or in the course of debugging a program, the output might reveal a possibility that could not be foreseen when the program was first planned.

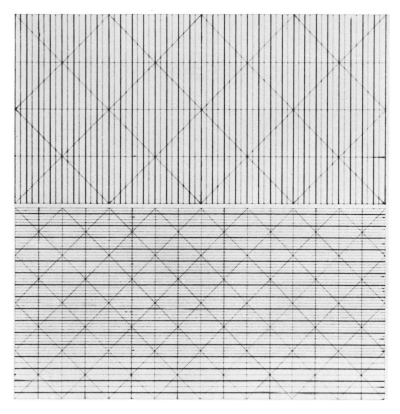

'4-Color Computer Graphic', 9¼ x 9½ inches, 1972.
A four-color plotter graphic made on the Amherst College IBM 1130
system. The program, called GRAF/D, was written in Fortran IV by the
artist. For making this drawing the program was run through twice, once for
the upper half and again for the lower half. Each drawing is one-of-a-kind.

However, I would hazard the generalization that the greater the power, scope, and versatility of a program, the greater the possibility of these unexpected discoveries. In fact, one of the delights of complex programs with many parameters is these surprising productions. And this also points up that one has to learn how best to use a program once it has been written.

"Could your work be done without the aid of a computer? If yes, why use the computer?"

My program GRAF/D does nothing but draw straight lines in grid-like patterns. I don't doubt there are thousands of artists who could draw similar graphics by hand if they were of a mind to. But I couldn't—or more precisely, *wouldn't*—because I'd either be climbing the walls, or making blotches on the next to the last line. Although this use of the computer can hardly be called cybernetic, it is still a sufficient excuse to use it. Mere convenience is a justification, just as we use machines to do many things we are able to do without them. But we use them nevertheless—and why not? And why not use the computer just for its convenience when making certain kinds of art?

TRPL is another cup of tea. In this case it would be plain madness to attempt to calculate, then hand-draw the precise scheme of lines and spaces required for generating the moire patterns that are so important to this series.

This same question might also be relevant to the three or four sculptures I made in the late sixties using TRAN2 as the program. Since these works appear to be rather conventional examples of abstract volumetric sculpture, it is difficult to perceive what role the computer played. But rest assured, it did play a role at the design stage, even though its contribution is not apparent. What is missing here, of course, is an output medium that matches the computer in its contemporaneity—something like holography, for example. In fact, I am still looking for that medium, and the delay in finding it explains in part why the punch cards for TRAN2 are resting on the shelf.

"To what extent are you involved in the technical production of your work, for example, in programming?"

At first I was unable to do any of the programming I needed and I relied mainly on students and paid assistants. But I have since learned some Fortran, enjoy programming as a designing and problem-solving activity, and wish I had the time to become better at it. And if need be I can pinch hit for Dave Backer, a student in the computer science program who helps me teach the Computer Graphic Workshop we have going at the University of Massachusetts.

When confronted with a really formidable programming task, however, I like to work with an expert. In this case my contribution is to specify the over-all character and purpose of the program, insist on some user-oriented features, and help in defining and naming the variables and parameters that are needed. By knowing something about programming myself I can work more effectively with the programmer.

But I have yet to come across any canned program or so-called graphics language that can do any of the things I am likely to ask of a computer (a possible exception is Ken Knowlton's EXPLOR, which I look forward to trying out now that it has been implemented on our UMass CDC KRONOS system). Occasionally I come across a program that I admire very much, like Jeff Bangert's simulation of the hand-made art his wife Colette was doing some years back. In this kind of situation I feel challenged to test whether I might obtain better results from the program

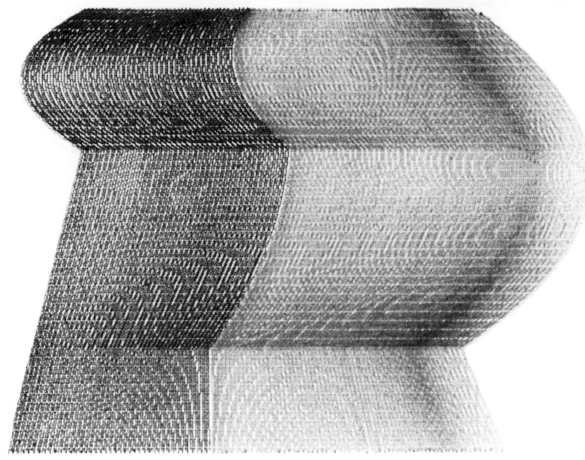

'2 Color Plotter Graphic', 4x5 inches, 1973.
A two-color plotter graphic made on the Amherst College IBM 1130 computer and plotter. The main program (called TRPL) was written by the artist. A curve fitting subroutine (called XFIT) was written by Dr. Roger Ehrich. The program interpolates a series of lines between a master line on the left and another on the right. A third master line is used to graph the spacing between the lines. The moire patterns result from the interaction between the spaced lines with a peculiarity of the pen, which is restricted by a system program to moving either vertically, horizontally, or at some increment of 45 degrees.

than its authors (in fact, I put the challenge to them once). Or perhaps results of the same high quality, but of a different character. However, the Bangerts are not about to let this program out of their hands, and I certainly don't blame them. This sophisticated program is much too personal to throw to the winds, or even to put into the hands of a trusted friend.

Those aspiring to a serious involvement with the computer should trouble themselves to learn something about programming, even if they have no intention of ever becoming experts. Nor does mastering one of the easy-to-learn graphic languages qualify anyone as a programmer. Real programming requires a close analysis and clear definition of the task to be performed, then an ability to design a program and devise the required algorithms. This is an intellectual discipline of the first order that has a potential in education beyond the technicalities of programming computers. I am also convinced it can play a role in the education of art students by helping them to think and discuss what they are doing more explicitly and analytically. At least, this is a major part of the philosophy behind our Computer Graphics Workshop and its teaching of Fortran to art students.

"Do you feel art work created with a computer has now or will have an impact on art as a whole in the future?"

Computer art has yet to make much of an impact, but it will. In fact, if I were not confident of its future I would not be interested in computer art, because the current level of performance is simply not that impressive. At this point I am charitable in judging both my own work and that of others (the question I throw back is: "What good is a baby?") But as time goes on standards must, and will, stiffen. Even now it is time to move beyond the easy gimmicks towards more substantial achievements.

"Do you intend to continue using the computer to create art pieces?"

Yes, even despite the constant irritation and frustrations of not having the resources to achieve what I know in my bones can be accomplished by means of the computer. Here again, I am inspired not by what is currently being done, but by what I know is possible.

"Do you recommend the use of the computer for others in creating works of art?"

Those who are right for computer art will find their way to it. But a minimal critical mass of information must be available and circulating. In fact, this collection of statements, articles, and material prepared for 'Artist and Computer' should help a lot.

Amherst, Massachusetts
November 1975

8

ALDO GIORGINI

'Negative Reflection', drawn with the program FIELDS written by Giorgini-Chen.

Dear Editor,

I hope you will accept my article in letter form. I think this device will allow me a freer hand than a normal article would, and, perhaps, a closer touch with the queries that you expressed in your call for papers.

My art background is, perhaps, somehow unusual if compared to the average American artist. At the age of ten, I was asked to apprentice to Carlo Ingeneri, a now well-known painter and sculptor of Decamere, Eritrea, who, to make a living, was teaching freehand drawing in the school I was attending. Initially my parents paid a fee which was later waived when my work in the shop was worth the instruction I received from the artist. World War II over, in 1949 my family moved back to Italy, where the same circumstance repeated itself. The freehand drawing instructor of the Scientific Lyceum I frequented in Voghera asked me to be his apprentice. Ambrogio Casati (this is his name) is a painter and sculptor who has worked in a number of media and has produced outstanding works which are now in high demand. He had been one of the handful of futurists that survived the ideologic condemnation of fascism and developed in a strong personal style that recalls both the Impressionists (for the subtle use of light) and the Futurists (for the special atmosphere of *in fieri* of his paintings).

Notwithstanding my dedication (I was spending an average of three hours a day in the studio) and my success in handling the media, I never considered seriously a future in art. The environment of my formative years (a mixture of maternal and paternal influence) had conditioned my order of achievement values roughly in the following order: Saint → Artist → Scientist → Hero → Builder → Politician and/or Moneymaker. A realistic assessment of my talents and the crushing conditioning of the above hierarchy made me choose engineering for a career.

Since entering college I have only occasionally produced some artwork, but the dormant interest woke up four years ago, when I started developing a wet technique with enamels and acrylics that took literally two years to control. I call this process *chastique* (from sto*chastic* tech*nique*).* The works done in this technique feature fantastic organic-like forms which, according to the words of Mario Contini, art critic of Eco D'Arte, Florence, Italy,

'The Kiss of Europa III', drawn with the program written by Giorgini-Chen called FIELDS.

---

*Friends of mine suggest that the name would be more appropriate for an intimate hygiene spray for virgins.

are "characteristically well balanced, refined, and stimulating at the visual-interpretative level. Urging ... masses full of meanings stand out from the background and arise as introductory archetypal data and as emblematic images, either for a free fantastical enjoyment or for an exclusively aesthetical fruition, *ad libitum*." I still work with this technique now and then, since I think that it is rich with possibilities for visual experiences, albeit I spend most of my time free from professional activities in the direction of computer visualizations.

As it may be suspected, I started using the computer as a scientific tool. In the years 1966-67, while Postdoctoral Fellow at the National Center for Atmospheric Research I worked on numerical simulation of turbulence. The research was very demanding at the visualization level and, therefore, I started playing with the output facilities for the best graphical representation of the results of my research. I made some computer generated movies with the CRT-microfilm facility of NCAR and in the waiting time between one output and the next I made some sequences

of didactical nature about Fourier Analysis. Once at Purdue, I had some graduate students in the same field, and I started 'playing around' with some of the computer drawings that were made as illustration of the research done. From here to the purposeful use of the computer as an art tool the pace was very short.

This being the origin of my computer efforts in art, it should not be surprising to discover that the way I use the computer in scientific endeavors has affected my thinking about its use for the production of art. In fluid-mechanic research by computer, the preparation of the computer programs and subroutines has always been seen by me as analogous to the design of laboratory facilities and of the instruments for physico-experimental research. I have called the complete set of programs and routines a 'numerical laboratory' for numerical 'experiments' in fluidmechanics. To be sure the time devoted to the design of the facilities and instruments (programs and subroutines) is of paramount importance, and sometimes one has to go beyond the conventional design for a true

'Claustrophobia', drawing made with the FIELDS program by Giorgini-Chen.

invention of instruments and facility parts. No matter how 'intoxicating' this design part, I've always tried never to lose track of the goal of the research: the experiments in fluidmechanics. The same attitude I have devoted to the 'computer visual experiments.' I have designed and invented programs and subroutines, not for their own sake but as components of the 'numerical laboratory' for the 'visual experiments.' You can see that this attitude is the same one that was implied in my mention of the chastique. In other words, in my view, programs and subroutines are the disposable part of the process of art by computer.

The prints that I send you have all been made using drawings generated with the program FIELDS, developed by myself with the help of Dr. W.C. Chen. These drawings (and some others not illustrated here) are the reason why the program was made. Other people may use this program, if they wish, (it has been published in its entirety with explanations for its use) but it must be realized that the 'numerical visual laboratory' called FIELDS, as any other program, is far less than a tool: it is literally a 'programme' with a large number of degrees of freedom for the user, but with a still larger number of degrees of freedom 'frozen in' by the designer. The user must realize that whatever output that program yields, it will reflect more the creative constraints of the designer of the program than those of the user. The user has to bend, to comply with a very general view of visual phenomena, and is bound to produce at best an original on the 'style' of the program, at worst a variation ➔ imitation of one of the existing outputs.

The word *style* has been used here with intentional critical connotations: the use of *one* program will guarantee the development of a 'style' (which some critics may discover as broader than the slogan-type styles which some traditional artists develop with the only non-ostensible purpose of being singled out from the crowd). In my view, this is a cheap way of getting somewhere with a minimum of effort. It is true that the development of a numerical laboratory for visual experiments is justified by the diversity of experiments that can be performed (in other words: let one day of creation be followed by six days of restful, complacent contemplation). But, in my view, these experiments should explore the region delimited by the degrees of freedom of the program, and not describe in detail the minutest variations that lead from one 'original' to the next. If one proceeds in the latter direction, a lifetime of stylistically coherent artistic production is guaranteed to follow the *one* day of creation.

With the above, dear Editor, I feel that I have implicitly answered several of the questions that you have asked. I will now answer explicitly some others.

"Do you have a final image in mind when your work begins?"

I think that this fundamental question should concern more the behaviorist than the art critic or the artist himself. But the question is asked over and over to any artist. He is, therefore, compelled in the direction

(a) of introspecting himself in order to discover his modus operandi;

(b) of reporting the eventual findings.

While the introspective phase may have its positive influence on the artist's conscious behavior, the explanatory phase may result in deleterious effects, since it may produce cliches that aim more at astounding than at reporting. (A propos, have you seen the recent television documentary by the title "Hello Dali"? Is his theatrical apparatus just a self-made gilded cage for the dead bird that a miraculous mechanism provides with predictable motion and *deja vu* melody?)

As an overly simplified model for the modus operandi of an artist I offer, semi-facetiously, the following continuum between the two extremes CeMO and MeMO.

CeMO (purely Cerebral Modus Operandi)—The artist *cogitat, ergo est*. Visual images are entirely manipulated ... pardon ... *menti*pulated by the artist's mind and the result of this process is transferred, by any convenient mechanism (the artist's hand, an apprentice, a construction firm, a computer ...), into vulgar material substance (Hello Plato!).

MeMO (Memoriless Modus Operandi)—The artist can react only to what he sees in front of his eyes, without any ability to mentipulate the visual images. The gestures that ensue (hopefully intentional) modify the subject of his visual stimuli.

I think that both conventional artists and computer artists may be found spanning the whole continuum, albeit (non-interactive) computer artists may find themselves closer to CeMO than to MeMO. In my particular case, when I am operating in the computer mode, I tend to fully prefabricate the images mentally and then to render them by computer. The complexity of some of my drawings (see Turbulent Communication) usually creates some doubts about this assertion, since they are very mediate elaborations on moire patterns. Nevertheless it may not be difficult to accept the fact that a relatively large number of experiments performed on the visual effects of moire patterns can give a rather intimate familiarity with the ingredients for their design.

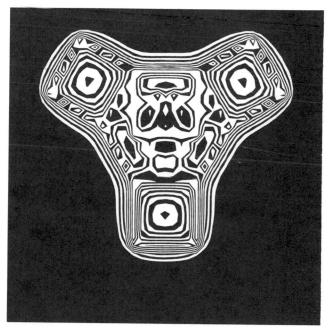

'The Kiss of Europa II', drawn with the program FIELDS written by Giorgini-Chen.

'Aldo Giorgini, X', drawn with the program FIELDS written by Giorgini-Chen.

"Could your work be done without the aid of the computer?"

Yes, in a fashion analogous to the one of carving marble with a sponge. Since all FORTRAN instructions could be performed by other techniques, there is no doubt that one could execute the same by calculating and drawing by hand on a Cartesian plane. The difference between the two approaches lies merely in the amount of time required for the execution of the piece. The time constraint is of paramount importance in all endeavors and we are talking here of time ratios that approach some orders of magnitude. The question, nevertheless, is amenable to another interpretation which is more immediate in the following formulation: "Does your work with the computer affect the direction of your results?" This question is germane to the other: "Are your computer works related to your non-computer ones?"

I strongly believe that any one artist using two entirely different processes will achieve two sets of results that are entirely different at the purely visual level. The only liaison between the two sets of outputs is constituted by the aesthetico-formal handling of the visual material and, if at all present, by the motive substratum of the artist's activity ("what makes the artist do it").

Since the purpose of this collection of papers is to present some personal views about (computer) art, I will devote the remainder of this letter, dear Editor, to the exemplification of the above concepts with the particular case of my own works.

The motive substratum of my artistic activity is constituted by the fascination that natural forms have always exerted on me: from the extremely complex organic forms, rich of life-like attributes to the geometric forms of crystalline formations and to the forms of the invisible fields around us. My mental projection of the visual elements that 'describe' natural forms is constituted not by their 'substance,' their being objects, but by the surfaces that delimit such forms. In other words, I am not interested in recognizable individual objects, but in recognizable forms, be they organic, straight-line geometric, or free-flowing geometric.

From this it follows that the selection of the processes for the rendition of such forms will be conditioned by the forms themselves. Furthermore, the intrinsic capabilities of the process will only focus on the typology of forms amenable to description by the process.

I end my letter, dear Editor, with the mention of my first one-man show. The show was exhibiting computer and non-computer work. The computer work was featuring black and white geometric forms, the non-computer work exhibited multicolor organic-like forms. Obvious contrasts. But to me the remark "They look like the works of two different artists" sounded novel and amusing. The schizoidal element is only superficial (like the one between the artist and the scientist). The 'motor' is one, and so is its formal creative apparatus.

My best regards,
Aldo Giorgini

West Lafayette, Indiana
September 1975

AARON MARCUS

I became involved with computer graphics in 1967 by chance when I was a graphic design graduate student at Yale Art School following an undergraduate education in Physics at Princeton University. I worked for a summer at Bell Telephone Labs then and continued afterwards as a consultant in computer graphics for a number of years. My art background is a life long interest and activity plus graduate professional study at Yale Art School. I have been continuously working, teaching, writing, and studying in this area since then. The computer is a tool for a simulation and stimulation of realities. At times it can become a useful 'partner,' but only in limited ways. I do the essential conceptual work and all of the programming. My computer-assisted works are definitely related to non-computer art, both mine and others, especially work in conceptual art. When 'work' begins I have schematic notions and images. These are finalized as programming and viewing develop. Some of my work could be done without the assistance of a computer, but it would be very time-consuming and difficult. Others, like my conceptual environments (e.g. 'Cybernetic Landscape I,' 1971-3) must use computer graphics systems to be real-ized. I have the ability to do my own programming (Fortran, APL). Luckily, too, because I am not a millionaire and can not afford a fleet of programming slaves. Also, luckily, because I like to

BAB CAB DAB FAB GAB HAB JAB KAB LAB LAB

Photoprint, 1972

make and learn from my own mistakes. I think much computer art (so-called) of the sixties and even today is constipated, trivial dabbling or merely ornamentation (see my article 'Computer Art: Towards a Second Generation,' *Print Review*, No. 2, Pratt Graphic Center, New York, 1973). Nevertheless, I feel it will have a much greater impact in the future as terminal/display equipment falls into the hands of everyone—both the consumer/viewer and the artist. I plan to continue my work in computer graphics as an art form and recommend that it (computer graphics equipment and education) be made available to others, especially in art and design schools.

Cybernetic Environments*

As writing was born, man struggled to find ways to compress his spatial, temporal, wraparound experience into abstract, easily reproducible marks on specially prepared flat surfaces. From essentially pictographic images bearing an iconic resemblance to things and actions, abstract forms evolved to provide man with more complex conceptions and a more intricately structured cosmos. After two millennia of relatively stable symbols and 500 years of their mechanical reproduction, the forms of writing, the ideas expressible by them are changing rapidly. At this moment, with the aid of electronic media and computer-assisted displays, the semiotic parameters of verbi-vocovisual communication are revitalizing long unused possibilities and discovering new combinations of elements for restating the inner and outer worlds of man's experience.

In the late nineteenth century, the poet Mallarme dreamed of a language and a language space in which everything could be expressive. With music as an ideal abstract formal system, he conceived of and began to make concrete a poetry in which marks, their form and position on a two-dimensional field, as well as their verbal denotations and connotations, contributed to a visual, spatial construction which one must see as well as read and hear. In the middle of this century, the international concrete poetry movement expanded and restructured the visions of 19th century innovators like Mallarme and Apollinaire. Joined to electronic, computer-assisted communication, the forms of visually oriented expression are beginning to bloom with a new array of ideas, a new dimension in abstract symbol communication and an all-encompassing environmental impact.

At the Computer Graphics Laboratory at Princeton University, I have developed a series of cybernetic landscapes utilizing programs in Fortran for a PDP-10 digital computer and an Evans and Southerland LDS-1 interactive computer graphics display system. The cathode ray tube device permits images in stereo and color as well as two-dimensional pictures which can be altered smoothly and instantaneously.

These landscapes in a simulated space provide a concrete, palpable, spatial experience of abstract visual forms and conventional verbal and typographic elements. As such, the space functions as a poem-drawing environment. Instead of the white field and black letterforms of traditional written symbols, the field is the deep, black space of night, and the symbols have been transformed

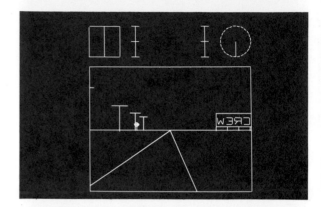
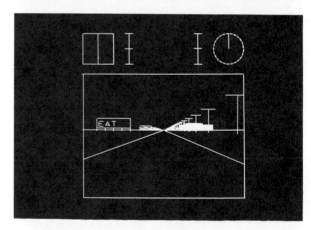
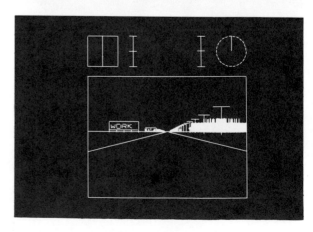

A sequence from 'Cybernetic Landscape I', 1971-1973.

*This article first appeared in the author's book, *Soft Where Inc.* It is reprinted by permission of the artist and WEST COAST POETRY REVIEW, 1127 Codel Way, Reno, Nevada, 89503 © 1975.

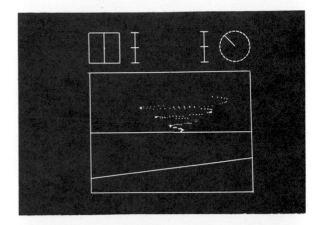

into glowing filaments of light—a direct extension of the desire for 'constellations' which Mallarme, Gomringer and others cherished. The 'objects' are diagrams for objects, as the letterforms are diagrams for sound/ideas. All are in a dematerialized form. Computer graphics effectively interfaces with man via light. The images have no mass, no physical substance in a sense, but they are perceivable and meaningful to the viewer. Most importantly, the statements appear in a three-dimensional space. The viewer/reader/participant is no longer bound to the flat surface of the incised, written or printed sheet. By using the interactive equipment (a 'joystick' and knobs to control the display), the viewer may look at and wander through this aesthetically composed symbolic space at will.

The illustrations show various views of *Cybernetic Landscape I.* The small diagrams at the top indicate location of the viewer on the groundplane (dot in the square) and direction of view along the groundplane (line in the circle). Bars indicate height above the groundplane and a vertical viewing angle. The space is organized with hortatory slogans of the Consumptive Good Life distributed along a sacred axis. At certain locations, other visual elements are to be found in the space away from the main path, and the viewer may explore these as desired. The simple forms near the center of the space symbolize the 'I' of the viewer—the vertical presence moving about the horizontal landscape plane. In one quadrant of the space is a kinetic piece, a whirlwind of letterforms rotating silently with a pulsating, varying rhythm independent of the viewer's position or movement. Within the space is a diagrammatic 'person' who moves randomly along the groundplane. This creature is both a 'mirror' of the viewer and an indicator that other viewers, other human beings, could be connected to this space, could 'enter' it and could 'meet' the present viewer 'inside' this electronically created environment. The space is cyclically infinite. Each side wraps around electronically to the opposite side so the viewer moving off one edge would emerge instantly into the space again at the opposite edge. To signal the beginning/end of the journey, a canopy of points/stars/periods hovers in space at one terminus of the path.

By means of this computer-assisted display, new relationships—new meanings—emerge, depending on the position, movement, and viewing direction of the viewer/reader/participant. As objects of light, the elements in the space convey a distinct and forceful presence combining the mystery of dreams, the awesomeness of the starry night and the wonder of the modern, man-made urban environment seen at night. Instead of the strict topology of the stele, codex and later book forms, the linking of elements can be richer and more complex; yet is achieved through visually simple elements: points, lines and planes. These visual components of our familiar forms have been transmuted into light and space. The reader travels through the text as context.

Princeton, New Jersey
September 1975

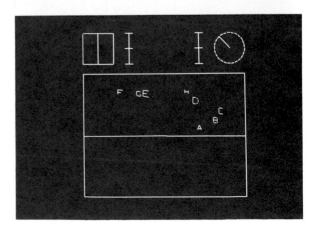

Various views of 'Cybernetic Landscape I'.

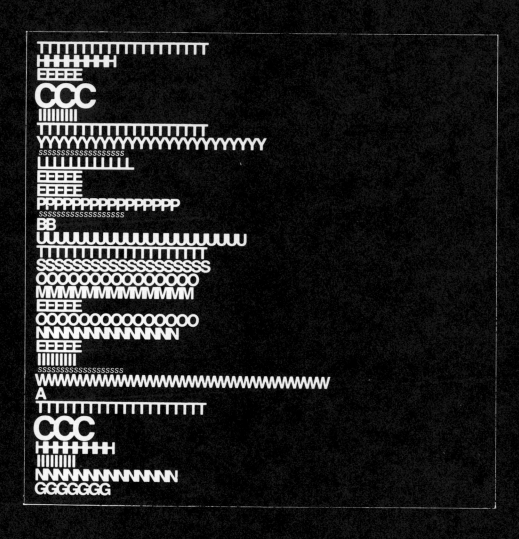

'The City Sleeps, but Someone is Watching', photoprint; 15x19 inches, 1972.

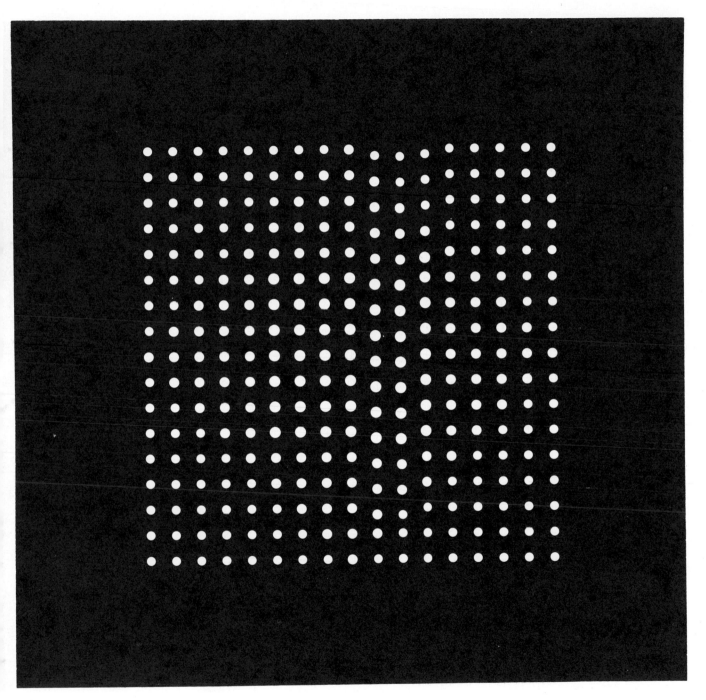

Photoprint, 1972.

COLETTE S. BANGERT

CHARLES J. BANGERT

COMPUTER GRASS IS NATURAL GRASS

Jeff and I have been making two-dimensional art for a long time. I've been making paintings and drawings since childhood and was educated as an artist. Jeff has been thinking what mathematicians think and writing it down since childhood and was educated as a mathematician and as an artist. In the 1960's Jeff became involved with computers and their programming and with using the computer to help people solve their problems.

When the University of Kansas was given a plotter in 1967, Jeff was asked to test it. We began to think of drawing lines with it in ways that we found visually interesting. Together, we had enough common background and experience to begin to use the computer graphically. Together we draw with the computer and sign the drawings CB—Colette-Charles Bangert.

The subject of all my work has been landscape. The elements of both the computer work and my hand work are often repetitive, like leaves, trees, grass and other natural landscape elements are. There is sameness and similarity, yet everything is changing. Landscape yields both texture and form. The pictorial form is usually all-over, with non-focus details which form patterns, since I feel these as essential properties of landscape. A field has no center, and is not really flat, so I use no flat areas. The form of grass as grass, leaves as leaves, is what I'm exploring.

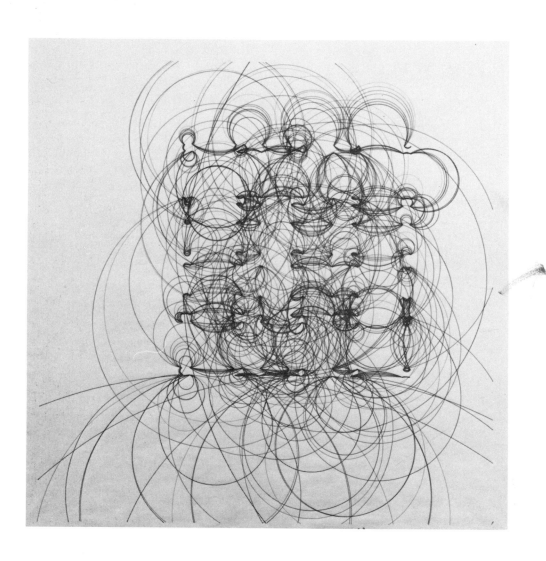

'Blue Circled Through Black' (continuous line study)
23 x 23 inches. 1972. Computer; colored inks on paper.

18

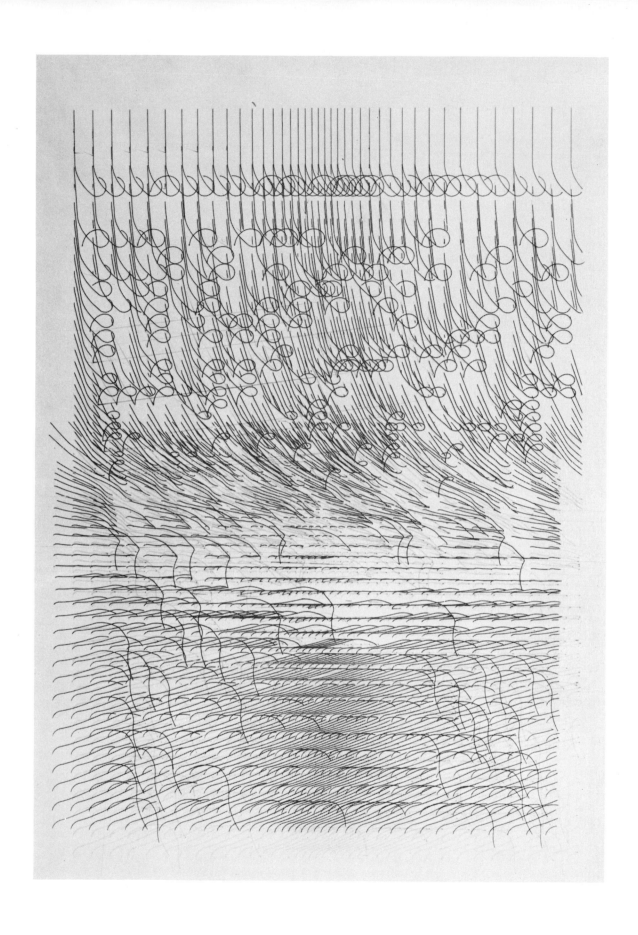

'Large Landscape: Ochre and Black'
33 x 23 inches. 1970. Computer; inks on paper.

'Contained Contours I'
8 x 8 inches. 197. Computer; ink on paper.

Landscape form is itself the subject. Line as form. Grass as form. Grass is also random and random is a natural computer facility. Computer grass is natural grass.

I always seem to be in the process of learning about line and land forms. I learn from what I see and what I draw. What my hand-eye draws is different from what the computer draws. A computer helps by offering new visual ideas. These ideas in turn enrich new hand work which generates additional ideas which extends my thinking about computer generated lines. The learning circle closes on itself. The computer and Jeff force me to verbalization and conception of what the making of a graphic drawing really is about. And I in turn force Jeff to think about the programming of serious aesthetic drawing problems. Together we try to define what makes up a drawing we would like to see. Without conscious understanding of what a drawing is we could not use the computer as a drawing medium.

A line carves out form on a white sheet of paper, a line carves out implied visual space. A line is an abstract element which I have seen and explored. A line is grass or the edge of a leaf, a shape, a symbol. The line does not exist, it can be drawn.

When we found that there was a device, a plotter which could draw lines, and a device, a computer, which could perform the calculations for driving the plotter resulting in lines which I only partly thought of beforehand, we found a very exciting but very difficult drawing medium. Using a computer-plotter extends my hand-eye-head. The computer draws, my eyes see, my hand draws, the computer is programmed by Jeff, the computer draws ... in an endless productive cycle. Computer drawn lines enrich my hand lines which in turn enrich my computer drawn lines ...

Jeff and I use the computer as a traditional drawing medium. The resulting drawings are to be seen, to hang on a wall, to communicate. They are not just examples of computer technology, not just geometry, not just mathematics. We ask this new medium questions and get new (and old) answers. But some of the answers were there from the beginning ... landscape. That it is possible to use mathematical formalism and pure geometry while attempting a humanistic exploration to us is one of the primary advantages of the use of the computer as a drawing medium.

Now I am beginning to see what a line is about. To see that I can choose to draw little lines, a one big sweep of the arm line, a coiled or an uncoiled line, crossing lines, spiraled lines, decorative lines, random lines, and it's all the same line. Where and how these lines are placed and colored make the drawing what it is, that composition is perhaps the truly difficult element in the making of a drawing. Now I have really to think about what I am doing while drawing in order for Jeff to write a program to deal with what I can do as second nature. This thinking has made the making of the hand work much clearer. We consider each drawing element as an independent element. This is artificial. Yet, this artificiality is precisely one aspect of the use of a mathematical attitude—the separation and isolation of individual elements of a problem. Our computer graphic efforts have shown us just how complex even the most simple meaningful hand made drawing is. In addition to making drawings using the computer, we appear to be finding out just what the making of a drawing is about regardless of its medium.

To me, the impact of the computer on the art of drawing will be profound. If I and Jeff and a computer can formulate visual ideas which communicate more clearly to ourselves and to others than just I alone can by hand, certainly the computer's effect on other artists will be even more profound. A new kind of renaissance is beginning. All those now working visually with the computer are Giottos announcing the coming of a new visual age. Just as the technical development of the camera changed people's visual experiences and changed art during the last hundred years, the computer will affect the visual dimensions of people's lives. The pre-camera, pre-computer Chinese artist took a life-time of understanding in order to make one meaningful ink filled brushstroke. It may take a life-time to develop a computer program to make one new communicating pen line which is meaningful for us.

Lawrence, Kansas
September 1975

BEN F. LAPOSKY

OSCILLONS: ELECTRONIC ABSTRACTIONS

My work in computer art is a form of oscillography, the results of which I have called 'Oscillons' or 'Electronic Abstractions.' These are composed of combinations of basic electronic wave forms as displayed on a cathode ray oscilloscope and photographed. Color compositions are achieved by means of special filter arrangements. The resulting art works are presented in photographic exhibitions, kinetic oscilloscope displays, light boxes, or movies.

The relationship of the oscillons to computer art is that the basic waveforms are analogue curves, of the type used in analogue computer systems. The oscillons have been recognized as being the first major development in this field as abstract art creations, and the first to be widely exhibited and published in America and abroad (over 216 exhibitions, 160 publications since 1952).

I got into oscillographic art through a long-time interest in art or design derived from mathematics and physics. I had worked with geometric design, analytic and other algebraic curves, 'magic line' patterns from magic number arrangements, harmonograph machine tracings, pendulum patterns, and so on. The oscilloscope seemed to me to be a way of getting a wider variety of similar kinds of design and with controlled effects to produce even newer forms not feasible with previous techniques.

My interest in other kinds of art was to some extent in abstract geometric painting, cubism, synchronism and futurism. The oscillons are related to the newer developments of op art, Lumia (light) art, computer art, abstract motion pictures, video synthesizer (TV) art, and laser displays, such as Laserium.

Oscillographic art might be considered as a kind of visual music, as the basic waveforms resemble sound waves. I used sine waves, saw tooths, square waves, triangular waves, and others in various combinations, modulations, envelopes, sweeps, etc. Oscillons usually are not accidental or naturally occurring forms, but are composed by the selection and control of the oscilloscope settings and of varied input circuitry. I used especially modified oscilloscopes for this work, as well as some of my own specifically designed electronic instruments.

The oscillons may be created without the use of an analogue or a digital computer system. It may even be possible, of course, to imagine or to compose some of these patterns without the use of the electron beam tracing them on the cathode ray tube. However, the electronic method greatly extends the possibilities of obtaining new and aesthetically pleasing figures. The oscillons are intended to be a form of creative fine art.

'Oscillon 3'

Objections are sometimes made that this and other kinds of computer art are 'machine art'—cold, impersonal, even inhuman. In some cases this may appear to be so, but it is obvious that the machines or instruments that form them are the products of imagination and planning, and at some previous initial point, the work of human hands. The output is conceived and controlled by human intelligence, and the results evaluated by personal aesthetic standards. If the computer is to produce art, it seems to me that the ability for it to do so must be programmed into it.

Cherokee, Iowa
August 1975

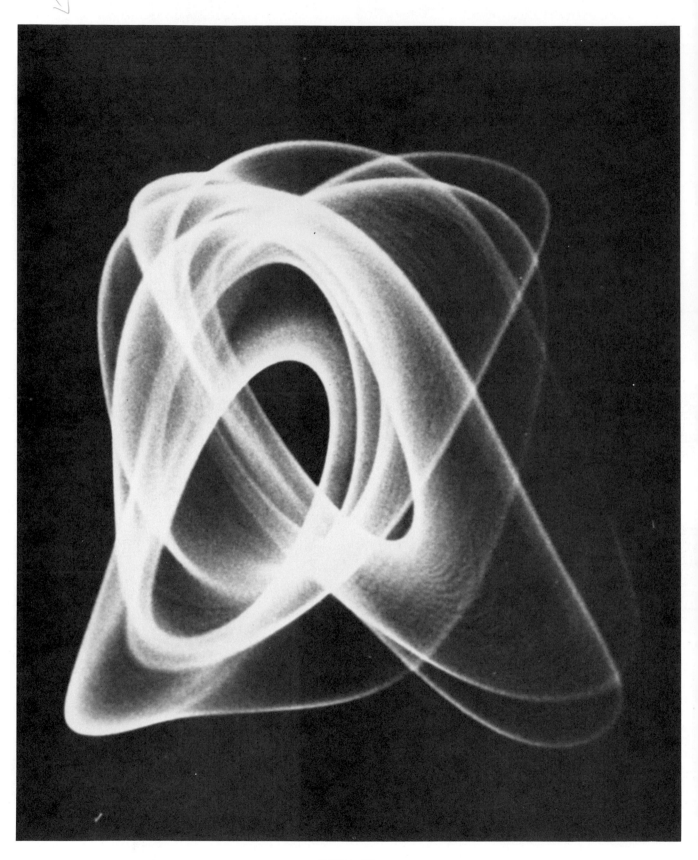

'Oscillon 45'

LESLIE MEZEI

Computer Art, as many new endeavors, has reached a plateau of stagnation after an exhilarating start full of promise. The computer specialists who first played with these possibilities soon exhausted their ideas and their interest. They merely did what was easy and obvious with their hardware and their even more limited software. Since they were first the results were unique and interesting, but generally 'artless,' and not very innovative.

The first wave of artists—really only a small ripple—that came to the computer expected miracles from it without a serious effort of learning and exploring and creation on their part. The results were in a way even more disappointing, except in the cases where the artist was already doing a type of art which could be directly assisted by computer techniques, such as modular art. Some instead succeeded in prettifying the output of their technical collaborator, without any real understanding of the processes involved. The rest were confined to existing programs and repeated the technicians and each other's work. Those first class artists that deigned to inquire into the possibilities were quickly discouraged by the lack of convenient control over the computer, the difficulty of communicating visually with it, and the amount of effort required to do it really well.

Today we are left with a small number of people from both sides, each of whom is aware of the long term effort needed to exploit the potential. The promise is as great as ever, but, as usual, requires more application and ingenuity and application than at first realized. The artists, and especially the art students, are willing to learn programming and some mathematics, and to learn to think in an algorithmic, process oriented manner. More importantly, in my view, they are ready to transcend the technological art so far pursued, and learn something of the underlying scientific ideas. [Applying any new technology slavishly results in imitative work, often foreshadowed by visionary artists long before the new technology. (Compare Picasso's drawings with some of our transformations, such as my BIKINI SHIFTED).] It is the new concepts and ideas, the new ways of thinking provided by the information sciences that will provide this. I am referring to our enriched understanding of system, structure, randomness and process as well as of the very process of communication and language, and the more realistic accounts of the methods of discovery in the sciences and the arts.

I have developed an Interdisciplinary course on the Concepts of the Information Sciences, in which we explore many of the concepts which come from cybernetics and computer science, communication theory and linguistics, general systems research and morphology, mathematics and operations research, etc.

The technical computer specialists, on the other hand, have to become aware of the potential contribution of the artists, develop a respect for their pattern perceiving and pattern generating abilities, for their trained sensitivity to the exploration of novelty, their ability to select what is most significant; indeed—at their best—to make concrete the future before it happens, before we can define it, formalize it and verbalize it. We may well end up in the next few years with a few individuals who have mastered both sides reasonably well. Programmer-artists and artist-programmers. Collaboration and multimedia are not impossible, only extremely hard and rarely successful. But then, so is most activity of a high ambition, high risk, innovative nature.

Of course, both should have an awareness of what has been already done, and what directions have been pointed to. My own book (Computer Art), which does just this is still making the rounds of the publishers, and the book introducing some of the information theoretic ideas applied to this field is in the German language ("Asthetik als Informationsverarbeitung," Frieder Nake, Springer-Verlag). Though Franke's book covers too large an area too superficially, it is the only book in English I can recommend ("Computer Graphics, Computer Art," H.W. Franke, Phaidon). In any case no exciting new ideas and results have appeared in the last few years; the next wave of creativity in this field is probably still a few years away.

What we ask of the artist is to use the science and technology to explore and expand our reality, and make statements of significance to today's tortured but expectant world. We have all filled pages and pages of programmatic notes, enough aims for a lifetime. Now it is time to raise the standards, to stop applauding the fact that we can do art with the aid of a computer at all, and apply as critical judgment to our results as to any other works of art. The

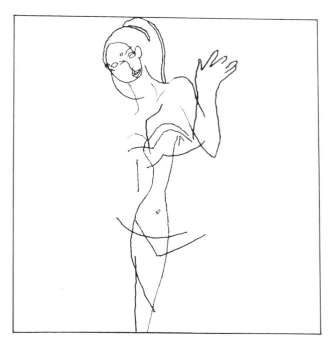

'Bikini Shifted'

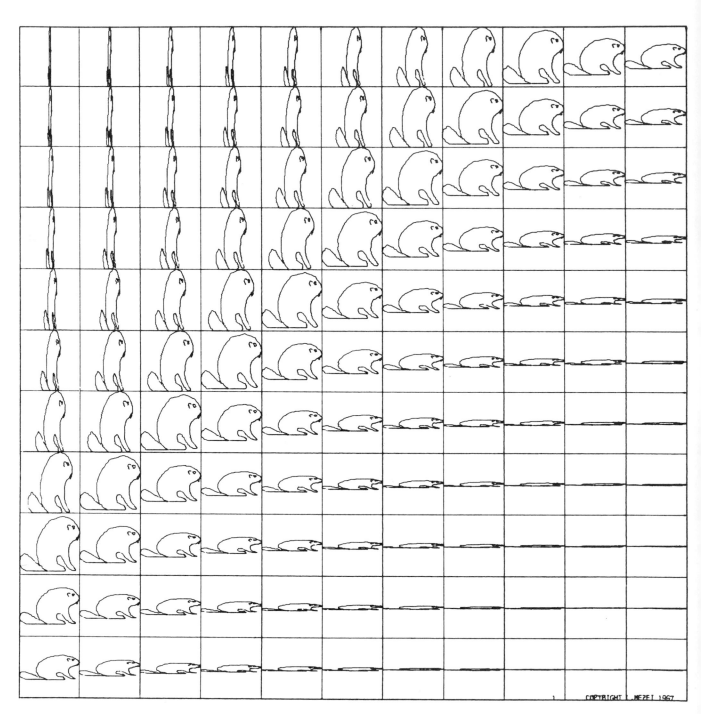

'BEAVER SCALED'

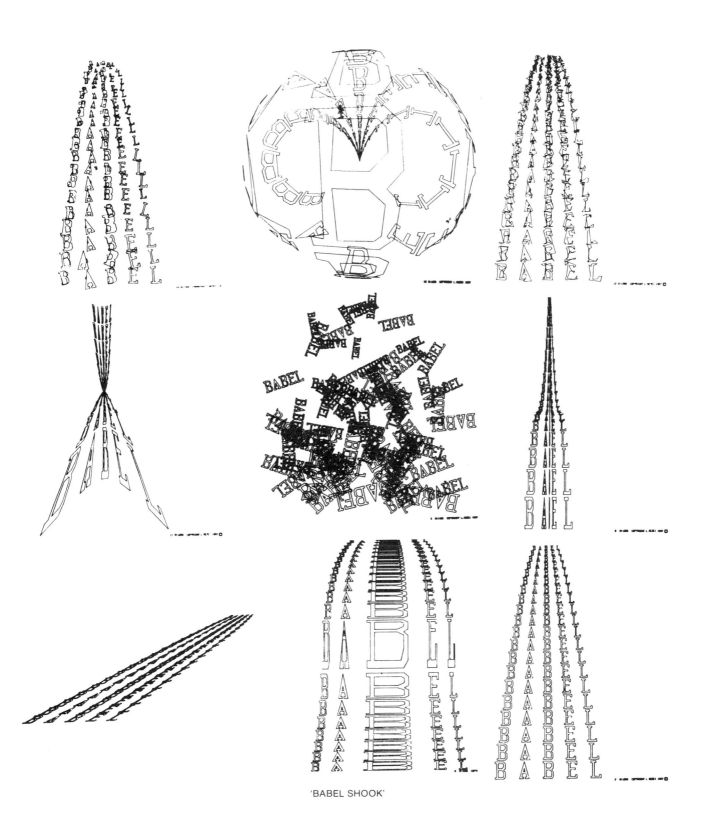

'BABEL SHOOK'

25

'SCALE of RANDOMNESS'

hardware and software are becoming more flexible and less expensive. Our own Dynamic Graphics Group, for example, is developing, under the leadership of Ron Baecker, a system with both a high speed line display and a digital color video tube, with sophisticated software for interactive dynamic graphics for artistic and simulation purposes. We are now making an arrangement with the local art college for a few of us each to 'adopt' one art student to work with us, sit in on our courses and develop themselves in their own way gradually.

My own work, all done a few years ago, has tried to make a novel beginning in the exploration of controlled randomness, of various distortions and transformations. These were neither systematic enough to be scientific, nor did they try to achieve the ultimate exploitation of their medium to be really good art. They merely tried to point the way toward new possibilities. From the still graphics I shifted to animation, and some successful films were produced on our system by a number of artists working with the help of a programmer. But I was not sufficiently involved with this work, merely the producer allowing it to happen. As soon as our equipment and software are advanced enough to undertake ambitious concepts easily, I intend to combine my developing understanding of graphic simulation methods and of the new concepts of feedback, structure, system, randomness and so on to try to create a new combination of science and art.

My background was in mathematics, physics and meteorology by training, and for the last 21 years computers, learned on the job. An early interest in the possibility of computer art (first paper on the subject in 1964) led me to become an academic, and to computer graphics research, as well as many other fascinating ideas and people. There is a constant struggle within me between the symbolic mathematical, the visual artistic and the verbal literary modes of expression, with the verbal winning at the moment. I do have a fascination with the visual possibilities, especially as seen in the incredible complexity and variety in nature—combined within many organizing aspects. However, to express this is—at least for me—a difficult, time consuming and indirect process.

We need to find those things which uniquely suit these new media, which can only be expressed with their help, and thus make the effort worthwhile. I look for the fresh wind of ideas from the new wave of art students who will be literate in the information sciences, and conversant with interactive computers and the new processes which they can help visually explicate.

Toronto, Canada
July 1975

TONY LONGSON

SIGHT AS A MOTIVATION

Sight is what interests me—in particular the richness of being able to see space—and this is what makes me make things.

The constructions I make are like drawings in space. They are made up of simple elements, such as lines and dots on clear sheets of material, which direct the way we see, and perhaps show us new things about the way we can see. Within these main aims there are other areas that interest me; the ambiguity of things that are flat yet appear to be three dimensional, and far more exciting, things which we know are in space which appear to be flat. I also like the distinction between pattern and not pattern; for example, recently I've been trying to spread small dots within a square in order to achieve a kind of 'grainy' surface. It's very difficult, I tried several random processes, but eventually had to determine precisely the pattern of individual dots so that no strong pattern groups were apparent.

This interest in sight as a motivation stems from the time I studied Fine Art at Reading University. Terry Pope introduced me to his 'extended parallax' glasses which, by increasing the distance between our eyes, dramatically heightens our impression of the space surrounding the objects we are looking at. I went on to build glasses which reduce the distance between our eyes, and was equally impressed with the new reading of space that they offered. It occurred to me then that there were many different possible configurations of two eyes which might provide exciting visual results. However, it was not until I came across computer generated stereo pairs that I realized I had a relatively simple way of checking all the alternatives.

'THEMES and VARIATIONS', 40x54x1½ inches.

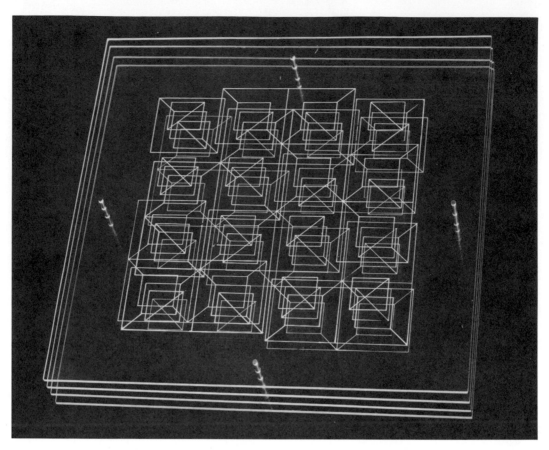

'GROUP THEORY GRID', 1972; 60x60x12 centimeters, PERSPEX.

So having turned to computers with that specific problem I began to see many ways in which they could extend my work. First of all I was interested in getting the computer to draw three dimensional objects. I set out to design objects which could be rotated into certain positions where they would appear to be flat. It was an interesting exercise as it made me aware of the many conventions we adopt, such as perspective, overlapping, and shading to depict space on a flat surface. Of course my first drawings were simple isometric projections. I went on to do exactly the reverse—that is to make three dimensional objects which appear to be flat from certain viewpoints. There was something attractive about seeing this unfamiliar situation.

Initially I thought it was enough to have someone else do the programming. Now I use computers in many aspects of my work (supported for two years by the Arts Council and Hatfield Polytechnic) and I find that I need to have control over every stage of the process. This means programming in FORTRAN, BASIC, and POP2 (more of that later), and being able to manipulate the various machines. Hatfield's main computer is a PDP-10, but there is also a small computer with a refresh display system and light pen which is connected to the 10. The majority of my work starts on this visual display, though not as an end in itself, rather as experiment towards making drawings in three dimensions. My latest sequence of work has been to investigate certain of the thresholds in the way we see. I enjoy visual information that will waver between two states, but never be both at the same time. I wanted to explore information that was highly structured, and yet at times seemed to be haphazard. I chose very small white dots as the elements to be seen against a black back-

ground. The geometry was to make a perfect matrix of dots within a twenty by twenty square, though as the dots could be on any one of the four separate layers which made up the drawing, that geometry would only be visible from face on. (Because of the diminishing effect of perspective, I made the dots and the matrix slightly larger as a function of their increased distance.) Added to this structure, I made the arrangement of dots symmetric about both horizontal and vertical axes (would that be obvious in the piece of work?). The square matrix was the only structuring that I wanted to be apparent in the work. From every other viewpoint the dots themselves had to have this grainy quality, that is, to have no local groupings which would be recognizable as strong patterns. This, of course, is the most simple explanation of something that has to be seen. The visual response that an object like this solicits is something that cannot easily be described. In the end, the whole is more than the sum of the parts.

To make the work, I've been using a numerically controlled three axis milling machine, which accepts information as co-ordinates on paper tape, and cuts corresponding lines or dots into the component sheets of clear perspex. It provides the necessary accuracy. Ironically mistakes are far easier to detect in visual information that is highly structured.

Well, there are significant problems in using a computer to creative ends; one obvious one is that the common output devices produce images with that characteristically dull quality about them. Also I find that each construction demands a totally new approach, and that rather goes against one of the fundamentals of a computer, the ability to repeat the same task reliably many times over; but what I see as their greatest limitation to creativity is possibly also

28

'DOT MATRIX', PERSPEX; 100x100x10 centimeters, May, 1975.

the very area of greatest potential. The limitation is this—a computer needs to have the problem closely described, and there are ingredients of creativity which cannot be described.

The potential, then, is to simulate the creative process itself. How can I do that? First I have to isolate those aspects of creativity which I do know about; simply recording them from my own methods. The computer has to have this information and non-numeric languages are available for expressing it (POP2 is one of them). Heuristics is a tested method for 'best bet' decision making where there are too many choices to investigate. And there is the kind of associative memory system which reinforces itself over a period of 'experience' of right and wrong choices. Hopefully this memory is common to an extended sequence of investigation. Given this situation, perhaps we can discover some of the mystery of creative thinking. I anticipate one serious problem. If the computer does make that kind of intuitive leap that we associate with being creative, how will I recognize it for what it is?

At least I am learning more about my own working methods—at best the computer may assist decision making in a naturally creative way.

Hatfield, Herts, England
September 1975

'WIRE CONSTRUCTION', 1972; 48x40x4 inches, PERSPEX. In the collection of the CON-GRESSGEBOUN, THE HAGUE, HOLLAND.

PETER STRUYCKEN

SPLASH 1972/1974*

*This article is composed of extracts taken from publications documenting the artist's work.

In the course of the last few centuries, particularly in Europe, the plastic arts have found their development in a personal, strictly individual sphere. In the first place people sought and still seek to express their emotions therein. The element of inspiration, intuition, vision or whatever men wish to call it, was and is essential as indefinable. Art is felt to be something comparable to a living organism, the substance of which can be defined, but the essence of which escapes every analysis. Yet it is true and recently the realization has grown stronger, in spite of all theories, that a painting or sculpture speaks to us in the

first place through visual means; visual means which are arranged by the artist in a specific interrelationship. The artist has worked this way and still does this more or less intuitively, so that in this arranging and handling of the material his personal temperament is revealed. Some artists, however, show an increasing tendency to banish the personal element from art in order to achieve an art which is determined by its own particular set of rules. Such an art would be placed above subjective preferences or concepts such as beautiful and ugly, because the work of art becomes the result of an indisputable, mathematical logic, which can only be qualified as true. However, such a work of art should not be labeled as inhuman, cerebral or sterile, since the longing for such an unassailable formula is very human; for was not this Plato's ideal of beauty?

I have searched for the elementary means of expression and I have formulated my findings in a set of propositions. It is my purpose to show that form and colour can be correlated mathematically; the result is not only a complete unity, but the interrelation of form and colour can be calculated as well. This might be of great importance when applied to town planning, architecture and industrial design. Thus, in town planning and architectural projects, the elements of which have a certain relationship as to size and form, it might be possible to apply colours which in their strength and tone acquire a corresponding relationship through which a complete unity of form and colour can be accomplished.

'Splash' is a program which allows the exploration of colour. The computer programme itself is just a number of logically formulated conditions. Their character is formalistic, they themselves having no content or meaning. When the computer programme is implemented, the conditions cause changes in the context of a previously established number of numerical values. These values are substituted by colour values when changes which they undergo during the course of the programme are made visible. A number, therefore, functions as a code for a particular colour. The number of colours corresponds to the number of numerical values. The result is a series of

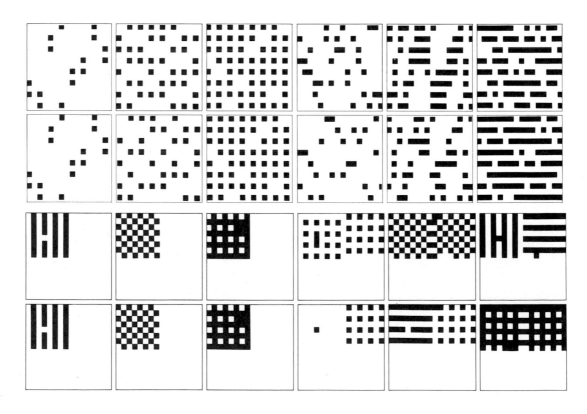

colour patterns which have undergone exactly the same changes as the numbers in the computer programme. For the sake of convenience the description of the conditions relevant for the programme always refers to 'colours' and 'colour patterns.' These terms can, if desired, be replaced by 'numbers' and 'number patterns.' The idea is to determine the quality of change, which can be big or small, sudden or gradual. The difference *between* the colour pattern is far more important than the colour patterns themselves; for it is this difference which indicates the *kind* and *degree* of change (which is the idea of this programme), the colour patterns simply appearing as 'pretty' or not 'pretty.'

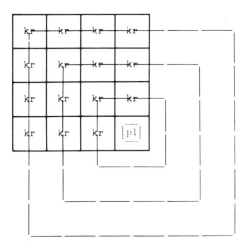

In order to have a rough idea of the way in which the differences between the colour patterns are caused, we can make the comparison of a stone thrown into a pond. Concentric ripples emanate from the place where the stone hits the water, the 'splashdown.' The larger the ripples become, the weaker the wave. The effect of the splash on the water is thus strongest in the centre, decreasing towards the edge. This image of a splashdown with ripples of decreasing strength can be applied to a colour pattern. Here, the centre of the change is referred to as the 'splashdown,' the colours arranged concentrically around the splashdown representing the resulting (square) ripples. In the first example (see fig. 1), the area indicated by the black lines is the pattern of colours which undergo change. *kr* means *kr*ing (Dutch for ripple) and *pl pl*ons (Dutch for splash). The grey lines indicate the position of the ripples which are formed around the splashdown but which are outside the actually visible colour pattern. The colour change is naturally strongest at the splashdown. The colours on the ripples around the splashdown change to an ever-lessening extent. The colour change is weakest in the outmost ripple, the one which is furthest away from splashdown. This is as far as the comparison between a disturbed surface of water and a changed colour pattern goes.

The computer programme which changes colours in the manner just described provides a number of transitional states between a previously (arbitrarily) established colour pattern serving as initial state and another previously (arbitrarily) established colour pattern which is to be the final state, or 'target.' The changes occur in such a way that the initial colour pattern corresponds to an increasing degree with the final one. An important condition is that as large a number of colours as possible change at once at one step. When it is no longer possible for the colour pattern to change as a whole in one go, the programme permits part of the colour pattern to change. When this is no longer possible either, the last possibility is for one colour per state to change. These various phases of change, together with their effect on the colour programme, form the basis of the programme.

Amsterdam, Holland
August 1975

EDWARD IHNATOWICZ

TOWARDS A
THINKING MACHINE

A great deal of discussion among computer-artists is centred around the question of whether the computer should be treated as a tool or as a medium, with some purists insisting that the term 'computer-art' should be reserved for the latter. The distinction may appear arbitrary, but it is in fact important because it distinguishes those artists whose inspiration comes from outside the world of computing and who use the computer simply for convenience from those whose ideas have originated as a result of computing experience.

My own involvement with computing began very much as a matter of convenience with a large, mobile sculpture being half completed before the possibility of using a computer was even considered, but the resulting experience has left me thoroughly entrenched in the computing field and apt to regard any present-day artist unfamiliar with computers with some concern!

The sculpture in question was built for Philips, the electrical firm, for their permanent technological exhibition in Eindhoven, Holland, and was called the Senster. It was completed in 1971 and took three years to build. It consisted of a sensing head comprising a moving array of microphones and two close-range radar transceivers borne on the end of a 15 foot long, articulated arm, powered by electro-hydraulics and controlled by a computer. The computer provided the machine with a certain behaviour pattern which on the lowest level tried to determine the location of any sound in the vicinity as well as the presence of any rapid physical movement and then to use this information to generate a movement of the whole structure. If the sound was persistent and below a certain intensity the movement was towards the sound, or away from it if it was too loud or accompanied by any violent gestures. This simple strategy resulted, nevertheless, in a very complex behaviour due partly to the complicated acoustics of the exhibition building and partly to the behaviour of the visitors who frequently surrounded the exhibit in large numbers and in the case of the younger ones, with a sustained din. The atmosphere around the sculpture was much more like that of a zoo than an art exhibition and I am sure that the majority of visitors would have been surprised to learn that the constructor of this machine had any pretensions to being an artist.

They may well have been right, since the title of an artist is an accolade rather than a qualification, but certainly my aims were artistic, as is my background. I had a standard art-school education (Ruskin-Oxford) and any technology I know is entirely self-taught and merely sufficient to carry out my designs. The involvement of artists in science and technology is not a new phenomenon since artists, like scientists, have been traditionally involved in investigations of nature, or more specifically, those aspects of nature which the current technology make accessible.

Speculation on the general question of what distinguishes the artistic approach from the scientific one are seldom profitable but perhaps a very personal view of such a distinction is worth making in view of the very technological nature of my work.

The scientists, it seems to me, tend to view the world as a vast, natural system, operating according to absolute and immutable laws which they try to discover by measurement and deduction, and they consider their own existence in it as being of no consequence. They are aware of the fact that all our knowledge is reducible to explanations of relationships within a floating frame of reference and are concerned about the difficulty of establishing a firm datum. In contrast, the essence of the artistic approach is to accept oneself as the only reference point and instead of explaining the world, to demonstrate the way in which it appears to one. This is not to say that such an attitude is a conscious one and that it exists at all is only an assumption. It is borne out, however, by the ease with which the work of most of the artists of the past can be accurately placed within its period and locality and even attributed to a specific person. It would seem that the artist acts here like a kind of anthropomorphic filter, choosing from the infinite number of possible aspects of reality those currently accepted as 'normal' with, perhaps, the individual deviations which at one and the same time identify him and constitute, often, his chief contribution. This 'normal' view of reality changes continually and is, of course, frequently affected by the current scientific and technological preoccupations and discoveries and thus is easily detectable in the contemporary art. Consider, for example, the impact on art of the discovery of perspective, printing, photography or the Newtonian theory of colour.

At the present time the effect of digital computing on our appreciation of nature is of fundamental importance and the area where the possibilities it offers are, to me, the most exciting is that of a better understanding of natural methods of control or development, growth, movement and behaviour in plants, animals and ourselves. The techniques of digital programming have greatly increased our appreciation of natural shapes and processes because instead of merely marvelling at their complexity, beauty or functionality, we are now in a position to consider the methods and techniques employed by nature in their generation. The popularity of Conway's Life game reflects this interest, as do many programmes written to generate shapes reminiscent of trees, plants and flowers.

Even more intriguing is the possibility of investigating and simulating the behaviour of complete systems, both natural and artificial and their responses to changing environments because this leads us directly into the realm of perception which, to my mind, is the central problem of intelligent life.

A great deal has been said about the research field known as artificial intelligence, most of it uncomplimentary and deservedly so in view of the many exaggerated claims and unfulfilled promises; nevertheless the understanding of understanding must remain one of the most inspiring goals of our civilization. This is a very new and uncharted area and many claims have been laid there by such scientific disciplines as neurology, psychology, linguistics, statistics and various computer sciences, to the point where the ambitions of any artists to enter the field may appear forlorn, if not actually presumptuous. The fact is, however, that no one has yet proved the suitability of any particular discipline for this type of investigation and, in view of the paucity of practical results, the game must be considered still open.

I should like to put forward a, no doubt biased, view of the difficulties which a purely scientific approach produces. The difficulties are to a large extent semantic in nature and have to do with the fact that scientists are fond of definitions, and that there are no satisfactory definitions for any of the relevant notions. Notions such as learning, perception, image, memory, cognition, knowledge, not to mention intelligence itself, are not in any absolute sense definable because they are all descriptions of relationships and attributes of natural systems and their environments. They can be demonstrated and appreciated more easily than defined or proved. If we can accept that a possible way of approaching the problem of cognition is through the study of the behaviour or artificial systems capable of simulating natural behaviour, then we must admit that there are very few guide lines for the design of such systems. Under such conditions it is at least

possible that an artist's open-ended, pragmatic approach may be of value.

What I am suggesting here is that even if we cannot describe intelligence we can certainly recognize intelligent behaviour and that the characteristics of such behaviour are such as to make them, in theory at least, demonstrable in an artificial system.

There is a commonly held view that even if the use of models of cognitive systems is a necessity, their actual, physical construction is not, since any such model can be adequately simulated in a computer. If accepted, such an argument would seriously undermine the usefulness of the proposed artistic approach since it is especially in the area of design and construction of physical shapes and control and interpretation of physical movement that the intuitive approach might be expected to be of value. Computer simulation has a serious drawback, however, in that it neglects the possibility of interpretation of sensory data by means of physical, ie. mechanical interaction, and there are good reasons for believing that such an interaction is the key element in the process of perception. It is difficult, in fact, to talk about the process of perception and quite impossible to demonstrate it without reference to some physical system, since the perception we are talking about is not the perception of abstract notions but of physical entities; it is clearly impossible to demonstrate an

'THE SENSTER', 1970.

awareness of a physical entity within a purely conceptual model.

Perception can be thought of as the process by which any cognitive system, natural or artificial, is informed about the state of its environment. It is not a measurable quantity and its existence in any system can only be established by an evaluation of its responses to the changes in that environment. Such responses are easiest to detect if they take the form of mechanical motion and this is one argument for construction of mechanical models. Another, and a more important one is that physical motion may be, in any case, a prerequisite of perception.

If we consider the possibilities of artificial simulation of perception, then a technique of measurement or comparison is a likely elementary candidate. This is because to perceive is to become aware of some property like size, colour, temperature or weight of some object or part of the environment or of the entire environment and this is only possible if this property undergoes a perceptible change or if another example of it is available. (If all the objects we ever saw were coloured blue we should not be aware of that fact.) Differences must be measurable and thus the process of perception is basically one of measurement or comparison. The problem is vastly more complex, of course, but the concept of comparison is a useful one because it raises the question of natural standards for what is to be considered normal. An autonomous artificial system should not have to rely on preprogrammed or hard-wired standards but be capable of establishing them independently. In such a case the only immutable standards available to it are some aspects of its own structure. It is conceivable, for instance, that a system capable of moving itself bodily and of sensing the force exerted in the process might be capable of forming a notion of weight by comparing this force with that required to, say, remove an obstacle. Similarly, a concept of length could be established by noting the distance travelled or the range of movement of a limb.

Conceptualization is, of course, another problem but it can be thought of in a similar way and considered as the result of correlation of two or more types of perception relating to the same object or entity. If, for example, a system can establish a definite correspondence between a set of visual data and a set of tactile data, a possibility exists of formulating a concept or an idea of the object to which these data appertain. Visual and mechanical perceptions are eminently suited to this role because they overlap in the all-important area of spatial and kinematic characteristics. Visual sensing informs in addition about the optical properties such as colour and transparency while the mechanical one about mass and dynamics, but both can inform us about sizes, shapes and movements of the same objects. In this way a concept can be seen to be not merely a perceptual record, but a means of complementing sensory data so that, for instance, an image of a known object may be elicited from its tactile exploration.

The important practical conclusion that can be drawn from such considerations is that the most basic type of properties that any cognitive system must be capable of perceiving is the mechanical one since it is through the consideration of the mechanical attributes that objects are most readily distinguished. The perception of visual images which is the most common form of perception we think of would seem to be much less important and only possible in conjunction with mechanical sensing.

One property of mechanical information which distinguishes it from most of the others is that it cannot be obtained passively. According to the quantum theory every form of measurements disturbs the quantity being measured, but it is never as apparent as when applied to mechanics. It is clearly impossible, for instance, to determine the stiffness of a spring without moving it. It appears, therefore, that the ability to perceive, or at least the ability to learn to perceive, depends on the ability to voluntarily disturb the flow of sensory information in a measured way which generally requires some form of physical movement.

This line of argument can be extended to include other types of information and is especially important in the case of vision which can be shown to be impossible in systems incapable of physical motion. This is well known to the psychologists who can demonstrate that cats, for instance, fail to develop an ability to see if prevented from moving during a specific learning period. That this should be so is easy to appreciate when we consider that vision is in general, and in the case of pictures always, a process by which a three-dimensional reality is reconstituted from its two-dimensional optical projection. Clearly such a process can only take place in a system capable of appreciating the properties of solid objects and, as we have seen, this requires an ability to move.

The area of interaction between optical and mechanical systems is in fact where the most exciting developments can be expected, but at the present moment the data acquisition processing expertise in the two fields is grossly out of balance. On the one hand we have very highly developed television technology, and on the other an assortment of electro-mechanical transducers and data loggers designed for simple measurements. What is required is a method of producing a mechanical image of an object rather like an image which we form in our mind when, for example, picking up an apple in the dark. Techniques for obtaining this type of information are not as yet developed and will probably require the construction of manipulator arms with sophisticated control systems employing either a large number of parallel force and vibration sensors, or a precisely controlled sequence of exploratory movements, or both. The even more difficult problem which needs to be solved is the method in which such information should be encoded. This is, to my mind, the central problem of artificial intelligence, but it is also one which may show us the way in which such systems ought to be developed. It boils down to the essential question of what intelligence is, and it may prove that it is the process of correlation of sensory and motor function in the way which may lead to the establishment of profitable responses and behaviour patterns.

In writing this I am aware of overstating my case and oversimplifying the issues in the interest of clarity in a manner which will irritate tidy-minded people. I am equally aware that this is not the place where such esoteric arguments will be proved or disproved. Like perception itself they will need to be demonstrated. I hope, however, that these rather self-indulgent musings may illustrate the way in which high technology and computing in particular is capable of affecting at least some artists.

If the above considerations do not constitute a design for a practical cognitive system, they may perhaps indicate some of the conditions under which such a system might evolve. They also constitute the framework within which I hope to continue to work and provide the criterion for the design of any other cybernetic sculptures.

London, England
September 1975

34

VERA MOLNAR

After an academic art school training (Beaux Arts) I began to make non-figurative images. The images I 'create' consist of a combination of simple geometric elements. I develop a picture by means of a series of small probing steps, altering the dimensions, the proportions and number of elements, their density and their form, one by one in a systematic way in order to guess what kind of formal modification challenges the change in the perception of my picture: perception being the basis of aesthetic reaction. My final aim, in common with so many painters of history, is to be able to create valuable works of art *in a conscious way*. Conscious way does not mean in my opinion the suppression of intuition, but its reinforcement by a cognitive process; it does not mean that painting becomes a matter of logic. Art at its inception is essentially intuitive, it is in its elaboration that intuition needs control and aid by cognition.

Since simple geometrical shapes are used, stepwise modifications are relatively easy to make. By comparing the successive pictures resulting from a series of modifications, I try to decide whether the trend is toward the result that I desire. What is so thrilling to experience is the transformation of an indifferent version into one that I find aesthetically appealing.

This stepwise procedure has however two important disadvantages if carried out by hand. Above all it is tedious and slow. In order to make the necessary comparisons in developing series of pictures, I must make many similar ones of the same size and with the same technique and precision. Another disadvantage is that I can make only an arbitrary choice of the modifications inside a picture that I wish to make. Since time is limited, I can consider only a few of many possible modifications. Furthermore, these choices are influenced by disparate factors such as personal whim, cultural and educational background, as well as ease of execution.

5 images out of the '196 squares series', 1975.

35

All these considerations are to explain why the use of the computer is imperative for my purpose. Using a computer with terminals like a plotter or/and a CRT screen, I have been able to minimize the effort required for this stepwise method of generating pictures. The samples of my work I give here in illustration were made interactively on a CRT screen with a program I call RESEAU-TO. This program permits the production of drawings starting from an initial square array of like sets of concentric squares. The available variables are: the number of sets, the number of concentric squares within a set, the displacement of individual squares, the deformation of squares by changing angles and length of sides, the elimination of lines or entire figures, and the replacement of straight lines by segments of circles, parabolas, hyperbolas and sine curves. Thus, from the initial grid an enormous variety of different images can be obtained.

I am working just now on a program whose aim is to explore systematically the possibilities of the program RESEAU-TO and to visualize in a exhaustive way all the types of images I can obtain. After my first approximate calculations I had 27,600 types of pictures. This number corresponds only to the *types* of pictures: inside of each of those types an infinite number of different images can be generated by changing the values of parameters one by one, several of them, or all at the same time.

It is obvious that this kind of work can not be done without the aid of a computer, and it is obvious also—as far as I am concerned—that my computer aided work is closely related to my former work carried out without the assistance of a computer.

This approach to the generating of pictures is not new; it had been applied long before computers were constructed. Making a series of pictures that were alike except for the variation of one parameter is not uncommon in the history of art (Haystacks and the Rouen Cathedral by Monet, for example). Just as erasing, scraping, retouching, covering parts of a picture or coming back to a preceding version were always familiar techniques used by painters. My computer-aided procedure is only a systematization of the traditional-classic approach. I believe that the use of the computer in art is an important tool for the working out of a 'science of painting,' more generally spoken of a 'science of art.' With regard to the impact the computer can have, I am in favor of the introduction of computer science in the Art School curriculum.

Tihany, France
August 1975

LAURENCE PRESS

COMPUTERS AND SERIAL IMAGERY

The reason I'm painting this way is that I want to be a machine, and I feel that whatever I do and do machine-like is what I want to do. Andy Warhol, 1963.

Rose is a rose is a rose is a rose. Gertrude Stein, 1922.

In his survey of serial imagery in paint[1], John Coplans defines serial imagery as "a type of repeated form or structure shared equally by each work in a group of related works made by one artist." This article will describe some of the ways in which I have used a computer to generate series of related images, but first let me discuss a few examples of serial imagery in other media.

The tradition of serial imagery in painting began with Monet who, being vitally concerned with light, often painted the same object or scene repeatedly under varying light conditions. Between 1891 and 1926, Monet painted series of groups of poplar trees, haystacks, the Rouen Cathedral, mornings on the Seine, Japanese footbridges, the Waterloo Bridge, and water lilies. Since Monet, many painters (mostly abstract) have worked serially. Andy Warhol, with his painted (and printed) series of movie stars, Mona Lisas, soup cans, coke bottles, etc. is the foremost serial artist today.

Serial imagery may also be found outside of painting. While Monet was doubtless motivated by a fascination with changing light, he may well have also been familiar with the photographic series of E.J. Muybridge, Thomas Eakins and E.J. Marey.[2] These were made in the 1870's and 1880's and often depict movement in an animal or a human athlete in a series of stills. Some of these are discrete images, separated in time by fractions of a second, and others are superimposed stroboscopic images similar to Duchamp's "Nude Descending a Staircase" or certain present-day advertisements depicting spunky, milk-drinking gymnasts tumbling about in red leotards. Today, one finds photographers such as Ray K. Metzger working with serial imagery.[3]

Larry Bell and Donald Judd are two modern sculptors who create series. Bell makes series of transparent boxes, each of which refract light in a slightly different manner (these are illustrated in 1). Judd makes series of identical modules which he might attach to a wall in a vertical 'stack' as well as series of objects which vary in size and/or placement according to some mathematical progression.[4]

Computers are well suited to the production of series of images. A series of identical images may be made by simply re-running a program, or variation from one image to the next may be induced by changing some parameter value with each run of the program.

I have experimented with series of line printer pictures made from single, digitized images. Each series includes an unmodified reproduction of the original and several copies which have been transformed along some dimension. For instance, a series might be made by reproducing an image with no random noise, with 5% noise, 10% noise … 100% noise. Before describing some of the transformations I've tried, let me say a few words about figure 1, which illustrates the mechanics of producing these pictures.

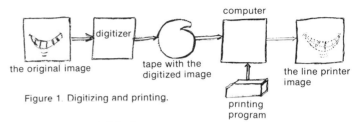

Figure 1. Digitizing and printing.

Digitizing and Printing

The process begins with a photographic print or negative which is automatically scanned and digitized. This is done by a machine which breaks the photo up into a 256 by 256 point grid and records the amount of light which is reflected back when a beam is focused on each of the grid points. If a grid point is in a very dark area of the image being scanned, little light will be reflected back and a high percentage will be reflected in a white area. The proportion of light reflected back is mapped onto a scale ranging from 0 (pure black) to 127 (pure white) and these 'light intensity scores' of each grid point are written on a magnetic tape. Scanning and digitizing an image in this manner takes about ten minutes.

At this point we have a magnetic tape with 65,536 numbers on it, which may be used to make any number of line printer (or other sorts of) images. The program to do this is fairly straightforward. Each row of the original is printed on a single line printer line. Varying degrees of shading are achieved by overprinting. For example to print a black grid point the characters O, M, W, and # would all be printed on top of each other; to print a grey point, the characters X and * might be superimposed and a white point would be represented by not printing anything. Table 1 shows the overprinting that I have used to get eight different grey-scale levels.

Grey-scale level	Printed characters
1 (white	blank
2	-
3	=
4	+,+
5	X,*
6	X,X,=
7	O, X, *
8 (black)	O, M, W, #

Table 1. Grey-scale overprinting.

Notice that there are only eight different grey-scale levels on the printed output, while each of the grid points was represented by a light intensity score ranging from 0 to 127. The most important parameters of the picture printing program are the 'clipping factors' which specify which parts of the range 0-127 are to be printed as grey scale levels 1 through 8. For example, one might specify

37

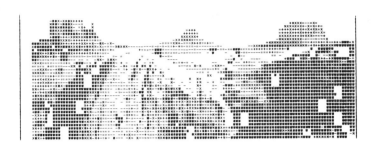

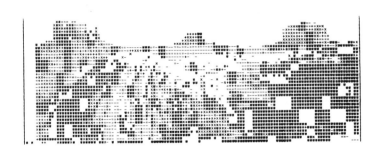

Compressed desert scene with correlated noise.

38

that all grid points in the range 0-48 print at level 8 (black), 49-55 print at level 7, ..., 100-127 print at level 1 (white).

Transformations

With these mechanics of digitizing and printing understood, let me continue with a description of some of the transformations I have used to generate series of related images from the same initial photograph.

1. Varying contrast.

Varying the clipping factors that are specified when an image is printed causes the degree of contrast in the print to vary. For instance, if one merely specifies that every point scoring above 150 print as white and every point scoring below 150 print as black, a high contrast, 'kodalith-like' image results. If the grey levels are distributed evenly across the light intensity range, a more 'washed out' image is produced.

2. Negative-positive.

By modifying the printing program to invert all grey-scale levels before printing (i.e. 1 becomes 8, 2 becomes 7, ..., 8 becomes 1) one gets a negative of the original. A single series may be produced which consists of a high contrast negative, normal negative, washed out negative, washed out positive, normal positive, and a high contrast positive of an image.

3. Varying noise level.

Random noise may be introduced into an image in a number of ways. For instance, the printing program may be modified to print grey level 8 points as grey level 1 with a specified probability p. If p were set to 0, a normal image would be made; if p were set to .10, the black areas of the image would be 'peppered' with white; if p were set to .5, a mottled texture would replace all black areas of the image; and if p were set to 1, all black areas would print as white.

Many variations on this theme are possible. For instance, I have tried leaving all white (grey level 1) points white while switching all other grey levels to white with probability p; printing a randomly selected grey level at each point with probability p; printing a randomly selected grey level at each point with probability p, but leaving all white points white; etc.

Regardless of how the noise is introduced, a series may be generated by simply varying the parameter p from image to image.

4. Correlated noise.

In the examples in the previous section, each grid point was examined independently and either altered or not altered with probability p. It is also possible to consider groups of points and alter the entire group with probability p. For instance, if one looks at 4 by 3 blocks of grid points rather than each individual point, the effect is to generate noise with a 'checkerboard' feeling. As with the single-point noise discussed above, many randomization algorithms are possible when dealing with blocks of points.

5. Smoothing.

The inverse of adding noise is to perform some sort of averaging operation to remove noise. For example, one could reduce noise by replacing each n by m array of grid points with their average light intensity score (if the entire array were replaced by just one point, the picture size would also be reduced). Another possibility is to find grid points for which the light intensity deviates by more than some threshold amount t from the average of the surrounding grid points, and replacing those deviant points with the surrounding average. Series of images are generated by varying the parameters m and n in the first example or t in the second.

6. Insertion of arbitrary material.

It is possible to print arbitrary textures of character strings at various points in an image. For instance, one can replace all areas within a specified light intensity range with some meaningful printed word. I have made pictures of Marilyn Monroe with the word 'ANDY' or 'MARILYN' inserted in all white (grey level 1) areas. Alternatively, some texture such as random noise, all black, all white, alternating white and black points, random white and black points, etc. may be substituted for areas of an image that fall within a specified light intensity range.

Another possibility is to insert words or textures in certain portions of an image regardless of the light intensities. The arbitrary material could be placed in randomly chosen spots, in the upper right hand corner, in one inch wide vertical stripes, in the center of the image, etc.

In any case, the results are more pleasing (to me) if the arbitrarily textured areas are outlined in white (grey level 1) points. In fact, regardless of how an image is transformed, white lines may be placed around areas of a given grey level, at random, or in arbitrarily selected areas of an image. This is another example of the insertion of arbitrary material.

In all of these cases, series may be generated by varying the amount and placement of the arbitrary material. For instance an image of Marilyn Monroe might be varied from an unmodified output to a few areas filled with the string 'MARILYN' ... to an entire page filled with the string 'MARILYN.'

7. Stretching and compression.

An image may be compressed by deleting rows or columns of grid points or it may be expanded by repeating rows of columns of grid points. A series might begin with a vertically oriented image that has been compressed to just a few rows of output, followed by successively longer images up to a copy expanded to perhaps 5 times the normal length.

Note that if rows *and* columns are repeated or deleted, the scale of the image is altered, but it remains in proportion. For myself, I prefer the distortion of proportion which occurs when an image is expanded or compressed in only one direction.

I was fortunate to get 'bootleg' access to the equipment at the University of Southern California Image Processing Institute for the experiments described above. Had I not been so fortunate, I would have had to pay $25.00 for each image that I had digitized and anywhere from $.50 to $2.50 for each line printer output, depending upon its size. (They were made on an IBM 360/44 which is fairly well print bound for all of the transformations that I've described.)

It is uncomfortable to be begging for 'bootleg' time. The problem is that computer art doesn't really fit anywhere. Neither computer scientists and computer science departments, nor artists and art departments generally take it seriously enough to underwrite experimentation. Perhaps this is as it should be, or perhaps the quality of our work will win a place for computer generated art, I think that the jury is (justifiably) still out.

Venice, California
October 1975

REFERENCES

1. Coplans, John, *Serial Imagery*, New York Graphic Society, New York, 1968.
2. Newhall, Beaumont, *The History of Photography*, Museum of Modern Art, New York, 1964.
3. Lyons, Nathan, *Contemporary Photographers, the Persistence of Vision*, Horizon Press, New York, 1969.
4. Agee, William, "Unit, Series, Site: a Judd Lexicon," *Art in America*, May-June, 1975.

MANUEL BARBADILLO

MY WAY TO CYBERNETICS

Sometime in the early Sixties I read a book by Norbert Wiener that had a big impact on me. I read it in Spanish, the title was "Cibernetica y Sociedad" (Cybernetics and Society).

The book impressed me because, in it, Wiener was dealing—although in different terms—with many of the very same problems that I was involved with at the time, which were related principally to freedom and automatism. Only the points of view were different; his was mainly an engineer's while my problems were of an artistic nature.

Some of those problems were then becoming clear in my mind, but others still were at a subconscious level. This latter fact was probably responsible for the profound experience reading that book was for me.

I know, from my own experience, that the important topics for one's development are those that at the time resound in one's subconscious. Because of that, I trust even isolated words, or single sentences that produce an emotional echo, more than coordinated theories, if these have no effect on my emotions.

Years later, when I had a clearer idea of cybernetics, and when my work was more developed, I realized that along with art's collective evolution—I had been making, on my own, the way to cybernetics. Or, rather, to a cybernetic vision of the world.

'TRIPTICO', 1966; acrylic on canvas - 3 panels - 66x66 inches.

Abstract-expressionism was by no means a sterile experiment. It has been one of the most important developments of twentieth century art. Its influence can still be seen in most of the subsequent trends. Including the very formalistic ones, for the development of art is dialectic, with the most fruitful symbiosis taking place precisely between radically opposed movements, such as, in this instance, an enthropic tendency and an organizational one.

In many respects this process is very similar to the scientific one, with Science penetrating step by step under the outer layer of things. In an anecdotal way I would even say that the divisionist process of the analysis of light, finally reaching the stage of 'Pointillism,' in painting, very much resembles the path of Science from the macrocosmic to the atomic conception of the world.

'BIONA', 1968; acrylic on canvas, 48x48 inches.

At the time when I read Norbert Wiener's book, my painting was reversing a shape-destructing process that had taken me from my initial realism to what has been known as 'Abstract-expressionism'—a style with complete disregard for shape and composition which placed the utmost importance in self-expression—and was beginning to build my new style on shape and rationality. This process, as well as some of my ideas on art in general, I have described in my article 'Materia y Vida.'[1] Mine wasn't an isolated phenomenon. The new emphasis on shape was a world-wide trend. Abstract-expressionism had been the end result of an attempt to produce an absolutely subjective representation of the world, as the image of the objective world—as our senses perceive it—had been destroyed by 'Impressionism.' Simultaneously, a trend which was started by 'Cubism' had been striving to set the basis for a new objective representation of reality— featuring our understanding of nature, rather than its appearance—through the development of new shapes and the attempt to establish their relationships.

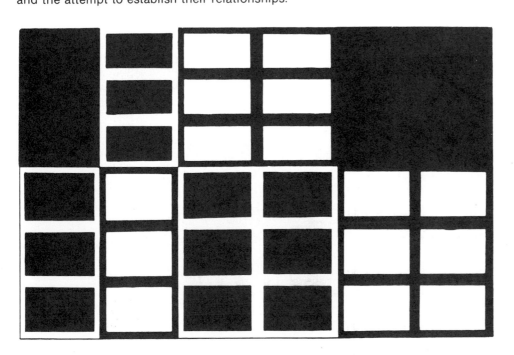

20x26½ inches, gouache.

41

'ANEYA', 1974; acrylic on canvas, 48x48 inches.

In 1968, I began computer research on my own painting, with the collaboration of the then newly-opened Centro de Cálculo de la Universidad de Madrid. My search for an objective language in my painting had led me already—through the practically total elimination of the subjective elements—to repetitions of a single shape in black and white compositions. I have explained my work with the computer in my articles 'El Ordenador,' published in the already mentioned publication, and 'Modules, Structures and Relationships; Ideograms of Universal Rapport,' of which a condensed version has been published in English.[2]

Currently, my work is based on a series of elementary shapes, or modules—four generally—which are the alphabet I build my pictures with. The definition of these shapes in a square is absolutely objective, and when repeated in a grid in various positions, they may originate an infinity of different designs. Their number depends on the squares in the grid as well as on the number of modules employed.

Starting with these modules, I try to express myself as the poet does with words or the composer with notes; by combining them so as to create a rhythmic pattern.

Basically, my painting is a research on the problem of space, which in my work is an element hierarchically equal to form, like a complementary form or antiform, in the same way that silence—pauses—in music, is a modulating element as important as sound, with 'form' being neither one or the other but the result of combinations between both of them.

In my pictures, space, rather than being a neutral element—a mere support for form—is a participating one, and the paintings, rather than of form and background, are composed of positive modules (black on white) and negative ones (white on black). This principle of oppositions and complementary opposites is essential in my work. It is present from the level of independent modules to that of very complex compositions. I believe it to be a statement on the bipolarity or dual nature of things, a notion antiquity held as the golden rule of the Universe.

The computer has been a great help to me. Properly programmed it will produce a great number of designs to study and compare, to choose or to get a stimulus from. It has revealed compositional rules I had been using in my pictures without being really conscious of them, and has allowed a great deal of systematization in my work. Since I use it more as a help for research than as a tool for execution, and am thus more interested in speed than in perfection of drawing, I prefer a line printer—with asterisks roughly filling the shapes—to a plotter. The final versions of my works I usually produce by hand.

Torremolinos, Spain
August 1975

FOOTNOTES

1. *Ordenadores en el Arte*; publ. by Centro de Cálculo de la Universidad de Madrid (Avda. Complutense s/n. Madrid) June 1969.
2. Page, *Bulletin of the Computer Arts Society*. No. 12. London, November 1970.

PATSY SCALA

WHY I BECAME
INVOLVED IN
COMPUTER-ASSISTED ART:
A STUDY IN
POETRY AND IMPATIENCE

I became involved in computers, as I became involved in art, through the back door: I have had no formal training in either field.

My work as an artist began with the writing of poetry, and through poetry, I was able to put onto paper feelings, ideas, everything which flooded my head, heart and body. With poetry, however, there was always something missing. As I wrote poetry, and, for that matter, as I did almost everything else I have ever done—drive a car, take baths, have a baby, have sex, teach—my mind was always flooded with visual images as well as verbal images. I had an uncontrollable urge to execute these visual images which constantly filled me.

There was, however, a problem with this. I can't draw. Nor can I paint or sculpt. I would attempt to produce an image in my head on paper, on canvas, and the image would somehow distort itself into a grotesque caricature of what I had wanted it to be.

I finally discovered, however, that through film, I could to some extent reproduce the fast-moving, brilliantly colored images that I saw in my mind, so for a while I worked in film. At this point, another aspect of my personality entered the picture: impatience. I hate to wait for *anything*, least of all a finished product of visual images I envision. I discovered that by the time I had completed a film, my mental images were very different than what they had been at the time I had conceived the film.

It was at this point that I turned to video, realizing that through this medium I could create images in real time. As I was seeing the swirling colors and movement in my head, I could record them on video tape.

I luckily became the artist in residence at the television studios connected with the S.I. Newhouse School of Public Communications at Syracuse, and was able to

'WIPEPOEM'—Fast-moving composition of swirling images created through use of analog-distorted refracted laser light, with added video effects and video color.

'Scope II'—Analog computer-controlled sinusoidal waves keyed in double image on top of one another, with special videographic effects added.

work with two two-inch high-band quadriplex video recorders, two film chains, three broadcast-quality studio television cameras and a highly sophisticated Sarkes-Tarzian control panel with two separate special effects generators. What a trip! I could sit at the control board and compose visual poetry in real time, as I watched my compositions on four color television monitors in front of me.

Even with all this wonderful equipment, however, I felt that something was lacking: truly varied input for my video-graphic pieces.

It was at this point that I became involved with computers. I attended a workshop given by Ken Knowlton at Eastern Michigan University. (I actually went there to go to a video workshop that was being held simultaneously with the computer graphics workshop run by Knowlton, but I discovered that the video work-shop dealt mainly with black and white porta-pak use, and that is not my style of video.) So stuck in Ypsilanti, Michigan, having paid my workshop dues, and having nothing to do but explore Ypsilanti, I decided instead to take Knowlton's computer graphics workshop. Reluc-tantly. Even though I had mastered the control of rather complex video equipment, the mystique of the computer had convinced me in advance that I could *never* learn to program a computer. I became violently ill, suffered severe stomach cramps, and fought continually with anyone I could find to fight with. Then a miracle happened. Ken convinced me that I actually *could* make a computer do what I wanted it to do. The rest of my stay in Ypsilanti is somewhat of a blur. My husband tells me that I had an affair with a PDP-10 computer, and he's probably right.

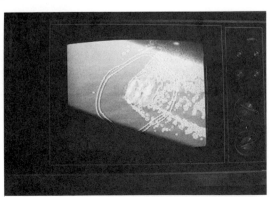

'Scope II'—Analog computer-controlled sinusoidal waves, with two separate waves keyed onto one another by the video keying process, put through a video feedback cycle and re-keyed, with analog chroma color added.

But it opened the door I was looking for: more types of varied images for my video tapes. I began to work with analog computer controlled sinusoidal waves shot on film, then distorted through videographic animation. I worked with my husband in collaboration on works involving computer imagery and video. I am currently in the process of collaborating with Stephen Levine from Lawrence Livermore Laboratory on more video tapes using computer input.

Now that I have discovered the computer, I don't think I will ever go back to other types of input to video, unless the supplementary input is combined with computer input.

My reasons? First of all, my video tapes tend to make a great deal of use of negative as well as positive space, and computer animation lends itself ideally to this type of imagery. Second, since I like images which can rapidly pulse, invert on one another, swirl, and burst out from an epicenter, the computer also lends itself to this type of imagery. Third, since my video art is still very much connected with my poetry, and I strongly believe that video images are a viable language for the writing of purely visual poetry, the computer gives me more options for visual diversity than any other single tool I could possibly use. Fourth, my impatience again. The computer can produce images rapidly, and this is very important to me.

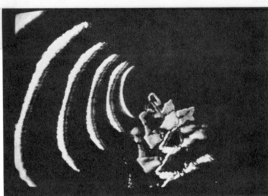

'WIPEPOEM'—Refracted light of red, green and blue lasers, distorted by analog-control, keyed three times through video, then put through a video feedback loop and keyed with video color added.

As far as I am concerned, computer art is going to be the catalyst which changes both the art world and the computer community. Once something has been done in art, the art world as a whole doesn't go back—even though some people will always go back to painting portraits of their grandmothers. Now that computers have become an integral part of the work of at least some artists, I strongly feel that other artists will begin to look at the computer as a viable tool for the production of art. At the same time, I believe that computer scientists are beginning to recognize that data they produce for scientific purposes can be quite beautiful. They—at least some of them—are becoming artists.

It could be a perfect melding of the many varieties of persons existing in our highly technological age.

Would I recommend the computer as a tool for all artists? Of course not—no more than I could recom-mend the paintbrush as a tool in my own art. But I would say that for artists looking for innovative images, artists seeking to find a place in their art for the technology which surrounds us, artists who are not afraid of machinery, the computer is a perfect tool.

Up with computers for artists!

Syracuse, New York
October 1975

WILLIAM J. KOLOMYJEC

THE APPEAL OF COMPUTER GRAPHICS

My interest in computer graphics began while I was an undergraduate working toward my Bachelor of Fine Arts degree in Industrial Design. I.D. concerns itself primarily with product aesthetics. I discovered when doing product design that many things could be quantified, including Man,[1] and that products might suit more people if they could be adapted or adjusted to individual needs. It became apparent to me that a computer which held the relevant data about a consumer could, during production, 'customize' an item and make it more desirable. This led me to further research culminating in a Master of Fine Arts degree in Graphic Design. This was unique in the fact that the majority of my endeavor was in 'Computer Graphics' making me the first 'computer graphic artist' to graduate from Michigan State University and, no doubt, one of the few Fine Arts people to have a minor in Computer Science.

During my investigations, I found a book with the dubious title, *Design and Planning 2*.[2] The book was largely based on contributions to the '1966 International Conference on Design and Planning' at the University of Waterloo, Waterloo, Ontario. It dealt with conceivable uses of the computer as a design 'tool' and gave specific to general explanations of design applications and possible design applications. For the first time the many nuances and ramifications associated with computer aided design were revealed to me. The appeal was so great that I had to investigate its use further and I have been involved with that investigation ever since.

The digital computer and peripheral graphic equipment (scopes, plotters, etc.) comprise my medium. I consider these things to be my tools and, as a Computer Graphic Artist, I must translate my imagery and desires into a form that can be used by this hardware. The medium is as complete and valid as any traditional aesthetic media be it painting, lithography, ceramics, photography or any other media. There are several strong similarities within computer graphics to these established media. Photography relies upon much specialized equipment in the total photographic process (i.e., from when the photographer composes or takes the picture to when the final image is printed and displayed). Computer graphics requires even more complicated and specialized equipment in its process of making computer imagery. Different configurations of computer and graphic equipment change output (the final form in which imagery is presented) and its similarity to other media. For example, with a plotter or hard copy unit, the medium should be considered as 'printmaking.' When a computer and a digagraphic display console with refresh capabilities are joined, computer graphics can be considered as cinematography. One final example would be three dimensional output. A computer and a numerically controlled machine, such as a milling machine, could produce a form of output which, for all practical purposes, would be sculpture.

The imagery of computer graphics can essentially be put into one of two categories with the possibility of having various ratios of these present in the final visual statement. The first category is the 'digitized image' where an image, be it representational or non-representational, is provided as data to the computer external to a computer program. The second method of supplying computer imagery is by means of algorithms, or internally as part of the computer program. The random number generator falls within this category. In my visual statements I employ both types of imagery. It usually depends on what I am trying to say or what I wish to explore that determines the method I use. When I have a specific representational image in mind, I use the first method and digitize the image. However, there are cases when the image, like a star or regular polygon, is more suited to an algorithm. In 'Banana-Cone,' figure 1, the key images of the banana and the ice-cream cone had to be digitized. Each image has 99 digitized coordinate locations and appropriate pen

KOLOMYJEC

figure 1: 'Banana-Cone'.

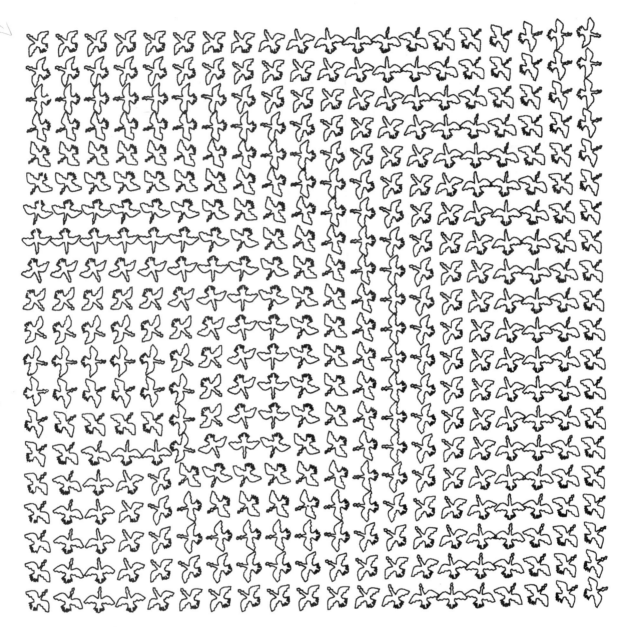

figure 2: 'Birds'.

controls for lifting the pen at proper line segments. The imagery originates from one of my wife's favorite treats, banana ice cream. That part of the process that takes an image between conception and symbolic representation is purely subjective and may come from many sources or personal experiences. It may also be a study of another work as I will explain later. As bananas can be made into ice cream to be consumed as food, it is possible to change the form of a banana using a linear interpolation into that of an ice cream cone which may be visually consumed again and again. If nothing else, the aesthetic method has less calories.

Other examples of using data bases of imagery external to a computer program are 'Birds,' figure 2, 'Bird Curves,' figure 3, and 'Creature Tunnel,' figure 4. These works are particularly good illustrations of one of the things that a computer does so well since the computer is very good at performing repetitious operations. These programs use the same data over and over again with slight modifications. To have done these without the aid of a computer

would have been too laborious and the quality of drawing would not have been as precise. I have put together a data base of four animals each having the same number of points and pen controls. From this menagerie I can select at will any, or all, of my creatures for use in a program.

Primarily I write my own FORTRAN programs. I feel it is necessary that a 'computer artist' do this. I consider myself a 'user' as far as the computer production hierarchy is concerned but I am neither an engineer nor computer scientist. Another thing I am not is a mathematician, but I sometimes work with one to help in writing complex algorithms such as determining the orientation of my imagery in 'Birds' and 'Bird Curves.' From writing general algorithms it is possible to piece them together as segments to make up other programs like 'Creature Tunnel' that does use several things including the total menagerie as its data. This program employs the random number generator to make decisions as to choice of animal, its position, and amount of rotation on a spatial cylinder. Finally all these things are put into perspective

figure 3: 'Bird Curves'.

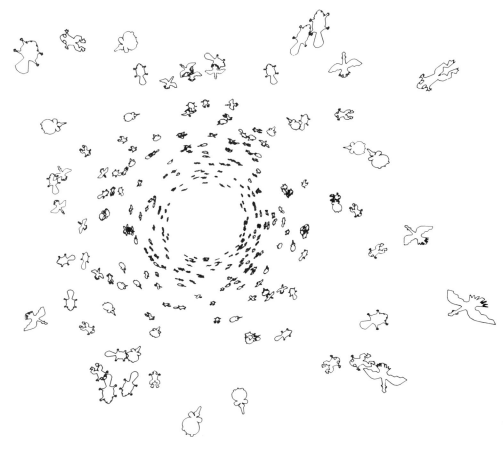

figure 4: 'Creature Tunnel'.

which can be varied and thus determine the final imagery. All in all, with so many options and combinations which comprise a program, the decisions which a computer graphic artist makes to yield a particular final image are identical to the decisions made by any other artists working in any other media.

The algorithmic method, or method of creating an image internal to a program provides imagery with a different quality. 'Random Concentric Squares,' figure 5, contains an algorithm that can divide an individual square within a larger array of squares into a random number of concentric squares based on the random location of a square with a fixed size located anywhere within its boundaries. 'Organic Illusion,' figure 6, uses the same basic idea of a large array of squares. However, its algorithm places a circle randomly with one square and equally randomly connects points to the extremities of that square. Note here that the points on the extremities of adjacent squares are coincidental and give a concrete overall structure to the work. 'Kolomyjec's Moire,' figure 7, deals with the optical phenomena produced by moire patterns. Considered as a group, these works have a similar quality about them yet they are dissimilar to the group of previous works. Using these works as examples, the distinction of these categories of computer graphic imagery become further apparent.

In my explorations dealing with computer graphics, I will, at times, attempt to interpret works of other artists. Just as all art students are impressed by works they have seen in the course of their studies, I too have been impressed. I enjoy making images that not only reveal the attributes of my medium but also exude the essence of those which I study. Figure 7, 'Kolomyjec's Moire' not only illustrates the logic of many branching-search algorithms used in computer science by computer scientists, it also may be classified 'Optical Art' and contains visual phenomena akin to that which an 'Op'-artist might produce. If we were to look at the works of the 'Op'-artists, particularly Richard Anuszkiewicz, Bridget Riley, and Victor Vasarely, one might be surprised with their similarity to computer generated images. Figure 2, 'Birds,' is a single image repeated over and over like Andy Warhol's coke bottles, soup cans, dollar bills, whatever. Yet I do not attempt to bring myself down to the level of the machine like Warhol, but rather try to bring the machine up to my level. I use more than just its ability to do

figure 6: 'Organic Illusion'.

repetitious operations, I also create a dynamic structure. There are other examples, however, I would like to point out a final one. A man who has been an unquestionable source of inspiration to me is Maurits C. Escher. The manner in which Escher derives imagery is so clear-cut and methodical that they seem almost algorithmic in nature. There is an excellent article about Escher in one issue of Scientific American magazine[3] that attributes his sources primarily to experiments on visual perception. Some of the techniques he utilized were naturals for computer imagery. His transformations of one image into another, 'Metamorphose,' 1939-40, compares with linear or parabolic interpolation similar to figure 1. His ambiguous limits of large and small, 'Square Limit,' 1964 and 'Circle Limit IV,' 1960, sometimes referred to as 'Heaven and Hell,' form interlocking structures of shapes while they increase or decrease in size and were my sources for two series of works: 'Homage to Maurits C. Escher' figure 8, which is the second from this series, and 'Escher in the Round' figure 9, which is the third from this series.

It is interesting to note that computer graphics as a 'fine art' had its first showing only ten years ago. In 1965 exhibitions of computer generated art forms took place in America and Europe.[4] The Americans were A. Michael Noll and Bela Julesz. Their European counterparts were Frieder Nake and George Nees. It was not uncommon for these early computer image makers to use the computer to duplicate a basic theme by a traditional artist. A classic study is by A. Michael Noll, 'Computer Compositions with Lines' 1965, after Peit Mondrian's 'Composition with Lines,' 1917[5] Figure 10, 'Boxes' in turn is my interpretation of a work by George Nees entitled 'Gravel Stones.'[6] I feel that it is appropriate to study works of other artists, especially traditional artists and those who established computer art in the fine art realm.

The computer has been labeled 'the ultimate creative tool for the artist-engineer-scientist.'[7] Computer graphics has the distinction that it allows an exchange between artist and engineer-scientist. The artist must work hard to learn the objective approach to problem solving, the engineer-scientist must acquire visual sensitivity and awareness. In a mutual setting, such as a classroom, both may exchange ideas but each must use whatever creativity he or she may possess to solve problems and produce computer graphics. Computer graphics exploits this creative potential in both artist and engineer-scientist. The

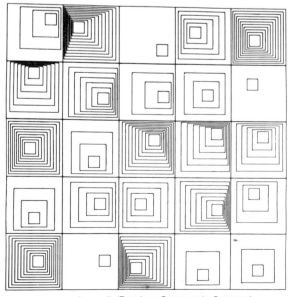

figure 5: 'Random Concentric Squares'.

figure 7: 'Kolomyjec's Moire'.

trend in recent years in art has been towards a collaboration of art and technology. Its roots lie in the Dadaist philosophy to alleviate the 'unrestrained individualism' of the artist. There have been many cases in art since 1900 where artists have 'physically and intellectually collaborated with new technology.'[8] The appeal of the machine has been overwhelming since the advent of electronics and electronic control. This is one reason why artists and engineer-scientists have gyrated closer and closer together. "… art as a whole (has moved) from depiction of movement to movement itself, from programming interface with the computer to the actual computer, from a lust for life to an involvement with it."[9] There is no question in my mind that art and technology have become willing partners and shall continue to influence each other in future. Computer art is a logical end in this involvement. Just exactly how it will affect art in the future remains to be seen. Yet there are some ramifications. It is possible to use a computer to generate unlimited unique multiples from one 'superoriginal.' I can

provide prints of figures 3, 4, 5, 6 and 10, each an original in its own right since each has the random number function built into its respective program. But some questions do arise. Is mass production of art by the computer the method to make art available to everyone? When produced in quantity, does the value as well as the price of art work decline? Are people willing to accept and support the computer as an instrument that can, under the control of an artist, be a valid form of individual expression?

As long as I can attain access to a computer I will continue to use it. It is my medium! Here at Michigan State University I have taught computer graphics as a form of expression for the past two years and the response has been overwhelming. Many art students, after an involvement with the computer, discover that there are objective methods to problem solving and any preconceived notions about the 'ominous' computer are dispelled, it becomes a tool in their hands. Many non-art students when they become acquainted with visual phenomena learn to 'see' their world under a different light. I

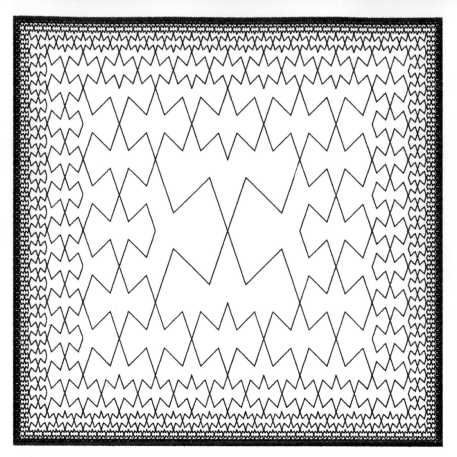

figure 8: 'Homage to Maurits C. Escher'.

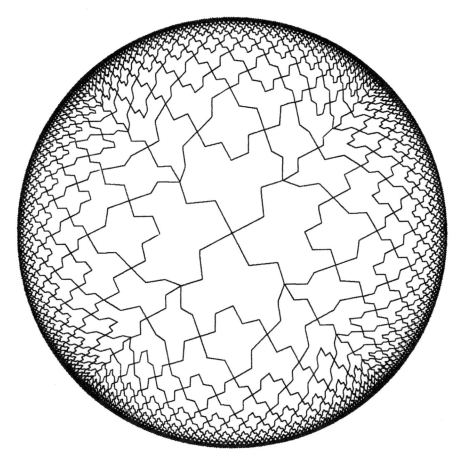

figure 9: 'Escher in the Round'.

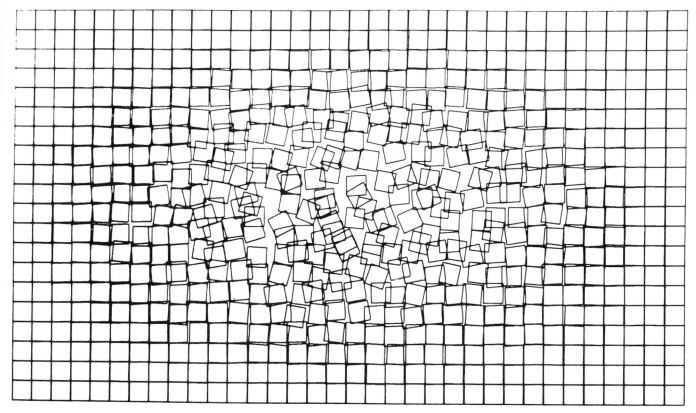

figure 10: 'Boxes'.

encourage my students to work together in debugging programs and evaluating imagery. All take part in classroom critiques. Here the collaboration reaches a maximum when artist and non-artist explain what thoughts underlie a particular work. The effort in making computer graphics is great but then so is the reward. I encourage anyone to spend the time and effort necessary in one's involvement with this medium. Perhaps the greatest return comes from the works themselves when the neophyte computer artists discover that embedded in their imagery is a little of themselves.

East Lansing, Michigan
September 1975

REFERENCES

1. *The Measure of Man*, Henry Dreyfus, Second Edition, Published by Whitney Library of Design, 1959.
2. *Design and Planning 2*, Edited by Martin Frampen and Peter Sietz, Hastings House, Publishers, Inc., N.Y., 1967.
3. "Sources of Ambiguity in the Prints of Maurits C. Escher," by Marianne L. Teuber, from Scientific American Magazine, Volume 231, Number 1, July 1974.
4. *Art in the Future, A History/Prophecy of the Collaboration between Science, Technology and Art*, by Douglas Davis, Praeger Publishers, 1973, p. 99.
5. *Computer Graphics—Computer Art*, H.W. Franke, Phaidon Press Ltd., London, 1971, p. 111, fig. 91.
6. Ibid p. 30, fig. 20.
7. *Art in the Future, A History/Prophecy of the Collaboration between Science, Technology and Art*, by Douglas Davis, Praeger Publishers, 1973, p. 97.
8. Ibid, p. 112.
9. Ibid, p. 112.

EDWARD ZAJEC

number of different combinatory strategies. This was achieved by introducing a determinant tendency which kept referring to a few basic criteria for guidance and qualitative feedback.

When the output of these programs was exhibited as stills in the form of computer graphics, I realized that the structure of the underlying process was of little or no relevance to the viewing public. This opened up a whole set of new problems which could be summed up by saying that no relevant contribution can be made by using the computer in the arts unless the public can be coinvolved as an active participant.

Computer graphics in this context merely represents a transition stage. They stand as stills in a process in motion and fall short of realizing the full potential of the medium. With a computer, we can now describe and communicate the organization, structure, and dynamics of a message. At the same time leaving it open to different interpretations and modifications, or better: only with a computer can we untie the constructive aspects of an idea from its material features and observe and articulate them in time through direct interaction.

This potential offers the possibility to develop programs which could actively involve the public and turn the passive spectator into an active participant. In designing interactive programs, some attitudes will have to be changed. The artist will no longer concern himself solely with the sublimation and expression of his internal world in the form of finished objects, but will have to deal with specific and locatable problems (even if hypothetical in nature) in order to be able to lend some of the control over to the participant.

I turned to the use of computers in 1968. At that time I was experimenting with redundancy in my paintings (repetition of the same module over large areas with only slight shifts in size). The monotony of the manual task and the limited number of variations which I was able to produce in a given time made me realize the inadequacy of traditional methods in dealing with our present reality.

At first I designed programs in which, given a basic repertoire of signs and a set of combinatory rules, the qualitative value of each possible combination depended on a predetermined balance between probability and chance. Later, I tried to extend the autonomy of the programs by developing systems which could produce a

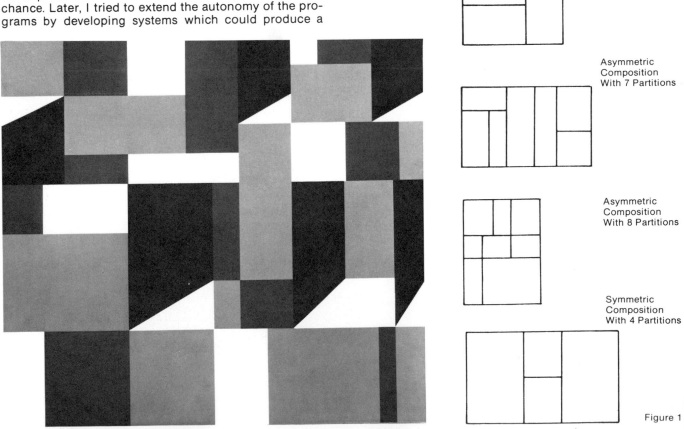

Asymmetric Composition With 3 Partitions

Asymmetric Composition With 7 Partitions

Asymmetric Composition With 8 Partitions

Symmetric Composition With 4 Partitions

Figure 1

'DIAGONAL WHITE 13685'

I feel that the main shift will therefore have to be from an object oriented art to an art which will emphasize those structural and constructive implications underlying a work or process which are not necessarily stipulated in its formal aspects (or in a final static result) and which can only be communicated in a direct interactive exchange. For example, we can gain very little knowledge about the structural and combinative properties of a system by examining the properties of its constituent elements in isolation. On the contrary, we must actually combine those elements to gain some knowledge about the range of developments which the system may offer. This means that instead of the traditional contemplation, the participant will be offered the possibility to engage in comparison, selection, and decision making; in short, creative participation.

Diagonal White

The procedure described below illustrates the latest version (Diagonal White) of a program which I have been sporadically developing since 1970. At this stage, it is an investigation of the combinatory possibilities of a set of non-determined modules, and of color, simultaneously considered as defining arrangements of differently colored planes, and as the representation of tridimensional space on a plane surface. The constituent elements of the system are: a vertical, a horizontal and a diagonal line for the definition of planes, the three primary colors (yellow, red, blue), and white, gray and black.

The new developments regard the formation of modules (spatial configurations or figures) which are no longer fixed or predetermined, and the color definition of the figure areas in function of their shapes. For this purpose I

the color choice for each area is random in the sense that different color arrangements can define the same composition without altering its spatial definition. The program develops through three separate stages which are functionally related:

Composition.
a) Define a rectangle whose sides will be determined by a ratio taken from the Fibonacci series.
b) Subdivide the given area into a number of rectangular partitions according to the harmonic proportioning mentioned above.
Notes: The initial rectangle can be subdivided either symmetrically or asymmetrically. The number of partitions is established by a random choice between a minimum and a maximum limit. (Fig. 1)

Figure formation.
a) Insert a matrix in one of the partitions (Fig. 2a).
b) Position a diagonal element in the given matrix (Fig. 2b).
c) Complete the diagonal element by extending a vertical and a horizontal line from each of its two ends (Fig. 2c).
d) Subdivide the remaining partition area into rectangles in compliance with the following rhythmic sectioning of the sides: 1,2, 2 or 2,1,2 or 2,2,1 (Fig. 2d).
Notes: The above is only a summary illustration of the figure formation process, since the number of diagonal elements for each figure, and the number of different figures for composition is determined in function of the

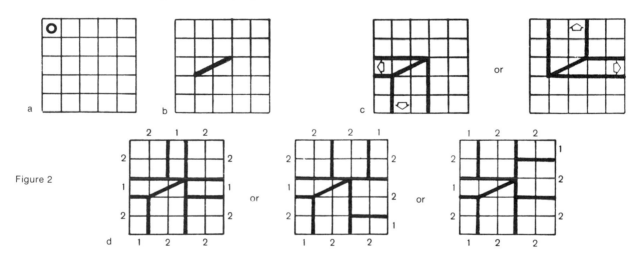

Figure 2

established an elementary, reciprocal relation between the shape of an area and its chromatic definition, which is exemplified by the following associative rule:
A rectangular area can be either yellow or red or blue.
A non-rectangular area can be either gray or black.

This rule complies with a basic criterion for which the coupling of the primary colors with orthogonal shapes defines flat surfaces in opposition to the coupling of gray and black with non-orthogonal shapes which gives an illusion of tridimensional space. White becomes, in this instance, an ambiguous element for spatial definition as a chromatic counterpart to the diagonal, since it can be considered either as one of the color tones or as the lightest shade in the white/black scale. For this reason it can combine with both orthogonal and non-orthogonal shapes. Therefore except for the definition of the white areas, for the associative rule mentioned earlier, and for certain qualitative tests regarding area size and regularity,

number of partitions and of the symmetry or asymmetry of the previously established composition.

Color definition.
a) Identify the largest non-adjacent rectangular areas, and apply one of the primary colors.
b) Apply a second primary color to the remaining non-adjacent rectangular areas.
c) Identify all non-adjacent non-rectangular areas and apply either gray or black.
d) All the remaining areas are to be white.
Notes: A general rule prevents areas of the same color to have one or more sides in common. When several areas with similar qualifications have common sides, priorities of choice are established by favouring larger size or regularity of shape.

Trieste, Italy
July 1975

DIAGONAL WHITE 75635

1) COMPOSITION

a) DEFINE A RECTANGLE WHOSE SIDES WILL BE DETERMINED BY A RATIO TAKEN FROM THE FIBONACCI SERIES:

b) SUBDIVIDE THE GIVEN AREA INTO A NUMBER OF RECTANGULAR PARTITIONS ACCORDING TO THE HARMONIC PROPORTIONING MENTIONED ABOVE:

SYMMETRIC PARTITIONING

TWO PARTITIONS

2) FIGURE FORMATION

a) INSERT A MATRIX IN ONE OF THE PARTITIONS:

b) POSITION A DIAGONAL ELEMENT:

IN CONSONANCE WITH THE TWO-PARTITION SUBDIVISION, TWO DIAGONAL ELEMENTS HAVE BEEN POSITIONED.

c) COMPLETE THE DIAGONAL ELEMENT:

d) SUBDIVIDE THE REMAINING PARTITION AREA INTO RECTANGLES:

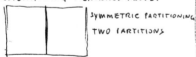

THIS SOLUTION DOES NOT COMPLY WITH THE RHYTHMIC SECTIONING OF THE SIDES, THEREFORE:

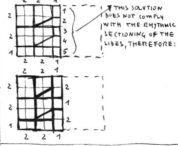

A SYMMETRICAL SUBDIVISION ALREADY IMPLIES A TENDENCY TOWARDS REDUNDANCY. THIS TENDENCY CAN BE CHECKED BY FORMING A DIFFERENT FIGURE FOR EACH PARTITION OR REINFORCED BY REPEATING THE SAME FIGURE THROUGHOUT THE COMPOSITION. IN THIS CASE THE REDUNDANT TENDENCY WAS REINFORCED:

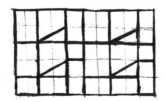

'DIAGONAL WHITE 75635'

3) COLOR DEFINITION

a) IDENTIFY THE LARGEST NON-ADJACENT RECTANGULAR AREAS, AND APPLY ONE OF THE PRIMARY COLORS:

b) APPLY A SECOND PRIMARY COLOUR TO THE REMAINING NON-ADJACENT RECTANGULAR AREAS.

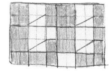

c) IDENTIFY ALL NON-ADJACENT NON-RECT. AREAS AND APPLY EITHER GRAY OR BLACK:

d) ALL THE REMAINING AREAS ARE TO BE WHITE:

The program was run on a CDC 6200 system at the Computer Center of The University of Trieste. The programming was done in collaboration with Dr. Matjaz Hmeljak.

'Diamond Variation II', serigraph;
1975, 32½ inches in diameter.
Ruth Leavitt

'SPLASH, 1972/1974'.
The beginning of a
splash sequence.
Peter Struycken

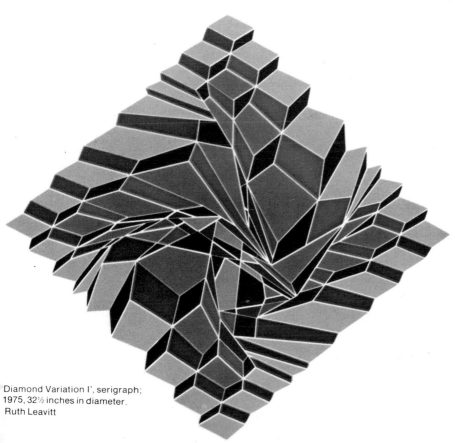

'Diamond Variation I', serigraph;
1975, 32½ inches in diameter.
Ruth Leavitt

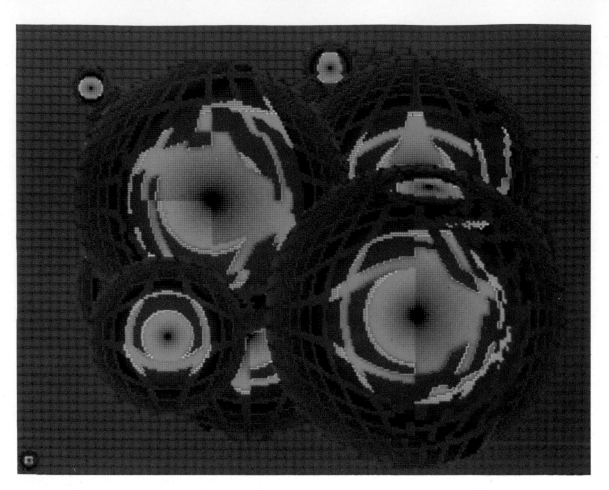

A computer Painting, 1975. Duane M. Palyka

A Bicentennial Tribute. Aldo Giorgini
copyright 1975 Aldo Giorgini

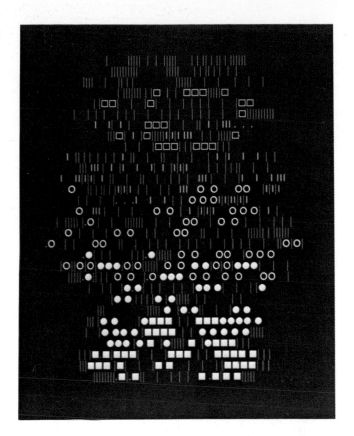

ades of Hades', lithograph; 5 x 6½ inches, 1972-4. Aaron Marcus   'Evolving Gravity', lithograph; 5 x 6½ inches, 1972-4. Aaron Marcus

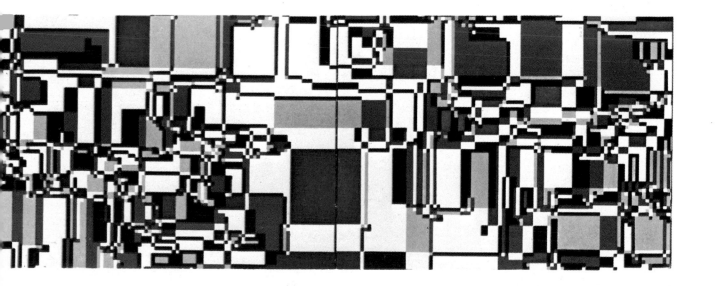

'Simulated Color Mosaic', Hiroshi Kawano

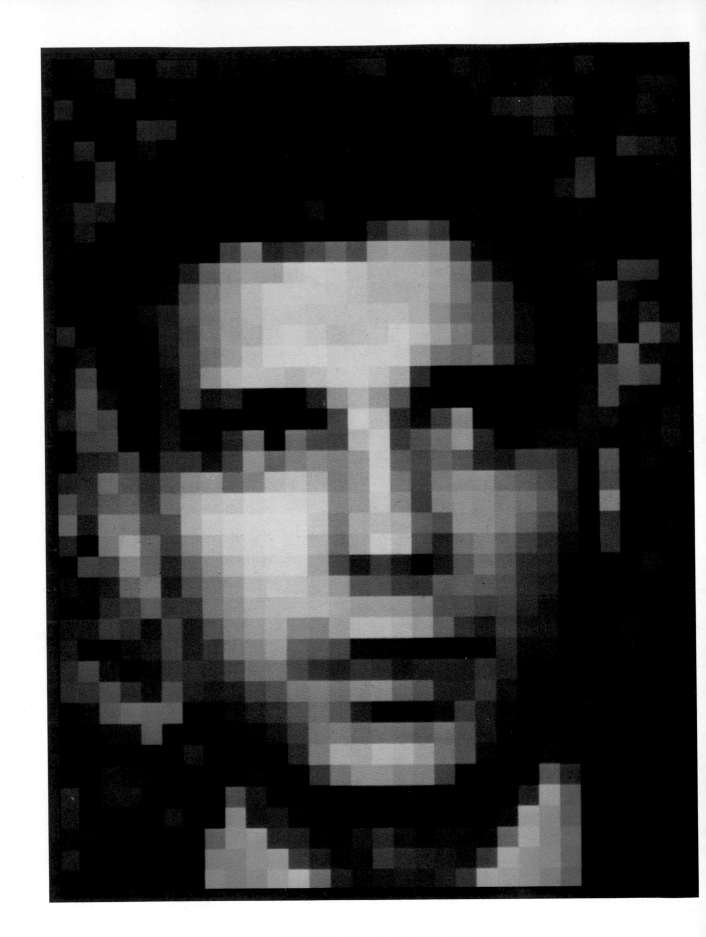

BLOCPIX™ of Ralph Nader by Ed Manning.

ED MANNING

BLOCPIX*

In the accepted sense of the word, the device I use is not a computer. It takes all of the information presented to it in the visual portion of the spectrum (as well as some outside) and, for a discrete area, integrates it. With ancillary sensing equipment, the device is part of a specialized computer. But that is another story and doesn't relate to the art form produced, so let me first answer your questions.

"How/why did you become involved with the computer (in producing art)?"

I became involved with the computer only in the sense that much of what I found printed and called 'computer art' lent itself very well to optical input material for colorful abstractions on the output of the optical processor I built.

"What is your art background?"

Although it was some time ago and I have difficulty remembering, I think I took art in the 4th, 5th and 6th grades. I could never get the hang of it. In my frustration I turned to mechanical drawing and was a skilled draftsman by the time I was 15 and I regularly produced model airplane plans for various model airplane magazines until I entered college.

"What role does the computer play for you...simulation, tool, etc? What is your role?"

In terms of Blocpix abstractions, the computer's role is to dish out some fancy patterns. Even though we can use the processor to make vapid designs colorful, the gigo principle applies.

"Are your computer works related to non-computer art?"

I don't work on a computer.

"Do you have a final image in mind when work begins?"

Some of the abstractions I have created are in my mind when work on the linear input program begins. The output seldom looks like what I had in mind.

"Could your work be done without the aid of a computer? If yes, why use the computer?"

It certainly can be done without the aid of a computer. But the computer produces a mass of material. Out of the mass, we try to elide the mess and use what's good.

"To what extent are you involved in the technical production of your work, for example, in programming?"

Not at all.

"Do you feel art work created with a computer has now or will have an impact on art as a whole in the future?"

Yes.

"Do you recommend the use of the computer for others in creating works of art?"

I couldn't be so presumptuous.

"Do you intend to continue using the computer to create art pieces?"

I intend to learn how to use the computer to create art, largely in connection with the Blocpix format.

My involvement with what I call Blocpix (which generically can be called block portraits) began at least a couple of years ago when I saw a news release from Bell Laboratories showing a picture of Abraham Lincoln in the block format.

The Lincoln picture was produced by a scientist at Bell Labs named Leon Harmon. I wrote to him, he wrote to me, and I made various suggestions. The picture he had created was produced by scanning an image, manipulating the digitalized information so that it produced an output of discrete tones for discrete areas...in this case, blocks or squares. I suggested to Harmon that the whole thing could be done more easily by optical methods. He said that he had conceived of an optical means of doing so.

Some months later Harmon showed me the output from his optical processor. Two pictures he produced were in the November 1973 issue of *Scientific American*. I made an arrangement with him to try to exploit the process in cinegraphic form.

At about this time, the very talented optical effects movieman John Whitney, Jr., produced about 2 minutes and 31 seconds worth of cinegraphic block portraiture for the Michael Crichton film "WestWorld". He did this very much in the same manner that Harmon had originally devised at Bell Labs. His operation was described in the November 1973 issue of *American Cinematographer*. Essentially, he took each 70mm frame of movie stock, color-separated it (3 basic color separations plus black mask), scanned each of these to convert into rectangular blocks. Then he added basic color according to the tone values developed and put the whole thing back together. We were chagrined when WestWorld was released and our idea had evidently been scooped. It was only upon reading the description of how he worked in *American Cinematographer* that we learned he accomplished what he did in such a difficult manner. To do the same thing with the optical processor would require about 5 minutes worth of filming.

As is readily evident from the 2 block portraits that Harmon prepared for *Scientific American* in the November 1973 issue, his device had imperfections. We had learned that a Frenchman by the name of Darnowsky was doing some similar work, and since I had considerable background in scientific instrumentation I decided to build an instrument myself. Because Professor Harmon thought that his idea was patentable, he had made no disclosure to me of how his processor worked.

As things turned out, the processor I built was, in principle, very much like Harmon's.

The device is simply an array of optical units each of whose cross-sectional geometry is square. There are 30 units by 40 units for a total of 1200. The unit produces results in real time...instantaneously...with an optical input, usually a projected slide. Obviously, you can project

*Trademark registered U.S. Patent Office by Watson-Manning, Inc.

BLOCPIX™ of Sen. Sam Ervin

motion pictures just as easily and photograph them on the output.

On the optical processor we make Blocpix images. Since the total output of the processor I constructed is 1200 squares, we're somewhat limited in what we can do. It lends itself readily to facial images. The information in a photo of a field of daisies is so overwhelming that all we get are beautiful blobs of color. On the other hand, a single rose looks like a rose.

Stratford, Connecticut
October 1975

DUANE M. PALYKA

COMPUTER PAINTING

Computer memory is an electronic surface—a thin sheet consisting of millions of small electronic elements called bits*, each with its own electronic field which can be measured plus or minus, one or zero, white or black. As these bits are set by a computer program, one can stand away from this surface and see clusters of bits, patterns of bits. These bit settings can form different gray levels, shapes, and visual images.

This is not totally imaginary discourse. A device called a frame-buffer was invented for just this purpose: to allow bits of a computer memory to reflect themselves on a visual device—the principal one being a color TV monitor. The computer memory is continuously scanned and displayed on the monitor; the way the bits are set reflects in the way the three color guns excite the phosphors on the tube surface. Programs can be written to change these bits dynamically and therefore give instantaneous color feedback on the TV monitor.

When a computer lends itself so easily to visual artistic exploration, why should it be restricted to engineering uses? Why should any separation be made between this and other artistic devices? The computer artist need not know about his medium below the plastic level any more than the painter has to know about the chemistry of his paints. The plastic level of the computer art medium, however, includes programming; but programming is just as plastic a medium in its own right as paint and brush, and can be thought of in a direct visual sense when coupled with an accommodating hardware device like a frame-buffer.

Both the creation of paintings and the creation of computer programs are the creation of objects—objects constructed out of ideas, concepts, and craftsmanship. The aim is a finished work with strong structure, patterns, imagery, and textures. A painting can be considered 'clean' if devoid of meaningless shapes and forms. A program can be considered 'clean' when the code has no meaningless instructions. Good structure in a program can bring as much esthetic satisfaction as good structure in a painting. The code and structure of a program reflects the personality of the person generating it. Both pro-

gramming and painting are problem-solving processes to which each person has his own approach.

Actually, in painting more emphasis may be placed upon the subconscious as the source of images and ideas. Not to exclude the fact that leaps of the imagination are needed to generate creative ideas in both media, programming is basically a logical process which utilizes an individual's conscious mind. Because of this difference, painting can reach a more mystical level of awareness—a depth of consciousness which we can experience but not explain. This does not mean that works of art are not logical, far from it. It is because the most creative works of art have such a logical basis that the computer fits in so well with the creative artistic process.

Take as an example Lewis Carroll's *Alice in Wonderland*. Few people will deny this to be a highly-creative work with imagery which reaches into unknown areas of our psyche, but this work is based heavily on strong mathematical logic taken to absurd levels. Lewis Carroll had a background in mathematics. On the art level, Cezanne's paintings have provided art historians with a source of analytical material for years, but so have Mondrian, Da Vinci, and many other painters.

An emphasis on logically conscious thinking is required with this medium to a certain extent since the computer works this way, but the computer artist's thought processes need not rest solely on this level. Programming is a step-by-step process where the programmer must understand what is happening at every step, but the images one makes using this process need not be totally 'understood.' The images themselves do not have a strict logical tie to the images which follow. The creation of images must have some logical visual flow from one to another to add order to the composition but, unlike the programming which generates it, the system of images will not collapse from the slightest deviation from logical conscious order. In fact, the deviations are what give emotion and tension to the piece. As in painting, with the computer art medium subconscious 'not-understood' constructions can co-exist with conscious 'well-understood' constructions. It is this aspect which makes art reflect everyday human thought processes and hence reflect life. Taking a computer scientist or a programmer who thinks continually on this linearly conscious level, it is interesting to see what works of art he prefers and what his view of representing the real world is. His thinking demands that he view the real world on a solely conscious 'understood' level. He makes strict comparisons between the images he generates and the world in front of him. In this attempt to render the world in this strictest sense he may even find it disturbing to look through two eyes when rendering a flat image because that means he has to choose which view to select, the one from the right eye or the one from the left.

It is interesting to note that as far as artists go, besides renaissance painters, Escher is one of the favorites. This is because Escher renders a reality on a very conscious level with deviations made on a strictly logical basis to keep it interesting. There is little leakage from the unconscious into Escher's images.

What this thought process lacks is the realization that leakage from the subconscious can make the images even more real in spite of the fact that they now deviate from the strictly-observable real world. This deviation personalizes the images by allowing the viewer's imagination to get in sync with the artist's on a 'non-understood' subconscious level.

Conversely, the artist could benefit from getting involved in linear conscious thought processes since it will give him more power in 'cleaning-up' his images and structuring his pieces. Through these processes he will

---

*A bit is the smallest numeric unit in computing. A bit can be either 0 or 1 in the binary number system. Three bits set 1 side-by-side make 111 (binary) which is the number 7 (octal or decimal).

have the tools to analyse his processes as well as the processes of others and help understand himself a little better. This experience can also assist in removing some of the irrational fears laymen have about computers.

Programming itself is filled with interesting visual imagery which, in turn, makes one think with new visual insight. Take, for instance, the idea of the 'bubble sort.' The bubble sort is a programming device for organizing a list of disorganized numbers into a list of organized numbers which increases (or decreases) sequentially. It does this by forcing the smallest numbers to bubble up to the top by means of a one-on-one comparison with the number above it. If it is smaller than the one above it, they change positions; if it is greater than or equal to, no change occurs. Imagining this process visually, it resembles the motion of bubbles. If one thinks in Paul Klee's visual terms, one can 'see' an implementation of this process on canvas. For the socially-conscious artist this concept can be expanded into the 'bubble-sort principle' to illustrate individuals rising in the business world according to their moral I.Q.

What is the overhead in learning the computer art medium so an artist can start thinking in terms of forms, shapes, and colors through numbers and programs? With paint, the first stroke one makes yields visual results. With programming, a person may expend many hours learning a programming language before ever really seeing a visual image produced with it. Unless the artist can get interested in the programming medium for its own sake, he can get discouraged and put an end to this business before ever getting started.

On the other hand, one can have the computer simulate a traditional art medium with which the artist is familiar and leave it to the artist to make the transition from the medium he knows to the new medium on his own terms. The computer is very good at simulation and, coupled with a frame-buffer, this particular simulation is simple to implement. Using an electronic pen and tablet for input, the artist can be provided with a medium similar to acrylic painting. He can watch on a TV monitor a flow of color reflecting his hand and pen movements on the tablet. In fact, he can even select the brush sizes he wishes to use.

An advantage that this medium has over acrylic paint is that the artist can change the medium to suit his own personal artistic needs through programming. As the artist learns to program he can see the development and change of his medium and, hence, of his images.

What kind of artist can get involved with the computer art medium? At this stage of the game, it takes an artist who can cope with dualities since he has to straddle two fields. He must have a flexible enough identity to accept the interflow of ideas from one discipline to another. He must be able to pursue what is interesting in spite of the labels that have been attached to it. He must be interested in developing both hemispheres of his brain—the half dealing with algebraic logic as well as the half dealing with esthetics. An artist who comes to mind who seems to have the flexibility to deal creatively with this medium is Marcel Duchamp. An artist capable in playing chess can become capable in programming computers. An artist involved in Dada or Zen can cope with the dualities. An artist whose ideas are conceptual as well as sensual can fit in well here.

The computer art medium can also help with the artistic risk-taking process. When an artist makes radical changes to his painting based on new thoughts and ideas, he risks destroying the painting to produce a highly-creative work. Giacometti and Matisse had the guts to wipe out hours of work to start afresh on the same painting. This can be a difficult thing for an artist to do. Giacometti developed a process of taking a painting to completion, wiping it clean, painting it again, wiping it again, etc. until he reached a state where he liked it or just gave up. A problem occurs when a previous stage of the painting had the best result but there is no way of retrieving it. Picasso found the desire to have two paintings developed to a certain identical state then each taken to completion in different directions. These tasks can be made easier with the computer art medium.

A digital picture, by its very nature, can be saved, transferred, and restored without any loss of information. To make a copy of a digitized image is to make another original. A bit is a bit and is transferred exactly. This means that an artist can save a state of his image, explore new directions in changing that image—perhaps a risky new direction that he was afraid to approach before, and retrieve his saved image to continue if he did not like the results of that exploration. This means that anyone with a compatible computer system can have the artist's work to do with as he wishes. In fact, the rip-off problems could cause some legal difficulties in the future.

The computer is also very good at repetitive tasks. A hypothetical program which would utilize this feature to the artist's advantage is one which would generate an infinite series of pictures, each created according to programmed rules of design coupled with algorithms or input devices which generate pseudo-random numbers. With a program like this one could actually satisfy the needs of the art world without boring oneself to death—creating enough similar works so the artist can easily be identified with a certain style.

Incidentally, because of the mathematical base of the medium, works produced with it could force the pseudo-mathematical approach to painting to assert itself in new and less ambiguous ways or die a natural death. An example of this approach is where the artist points to a triangle on his canvas and tries to imply a mystical mathematical base to the work by stating that one point of his triangle is 'A,' another is 'B,' etc. without reaching any definitive depth on the matter. To be ambiguous is a natural part of the art process for reasons explained above. No one is really expected to explain a work of art. However, to be ambiguous when making a correlation between an art object and mathematics is placing oneself on dangerous grounds.

Every case mentioned above has the artist working alone to create his images. Why not have the artist work with a programmer to produce his images? The artist-programmer relationship can be a learning process for both individuals; each finds out more about how the other thinks. However, if we view the situation according to the quality of art work produced, and if we make the assumptions that the programmer is not an artist and that the artist is not a programmer, the following two problems occur.

First, the artist uses the programmer as a tool to produce his art. In the process of providing the artist with a higher level between him and the machine, the programmer becomes an extension of the machine in the sense that his work is also included in the area of the black box. This is fine for having the computer simulate a calculator, but not so good for trying to produce creative work on a more personal level.

Second, since the artist's ideas about what the computer can do are sketchy and since his own ideas about what he wants the computer to do are not defined well enough in a common language that both understand, a lack of communication occurs which prevents any real depth of image-making to occur. The scientific process and the artistic process differ on one basic point: the artist allows feedback from the process to dictate changes in his goals whereas the scientist will interpret his feedback as defining a state of his progress towards his predefined goals. Consequently, at the start of the process, the artist has a

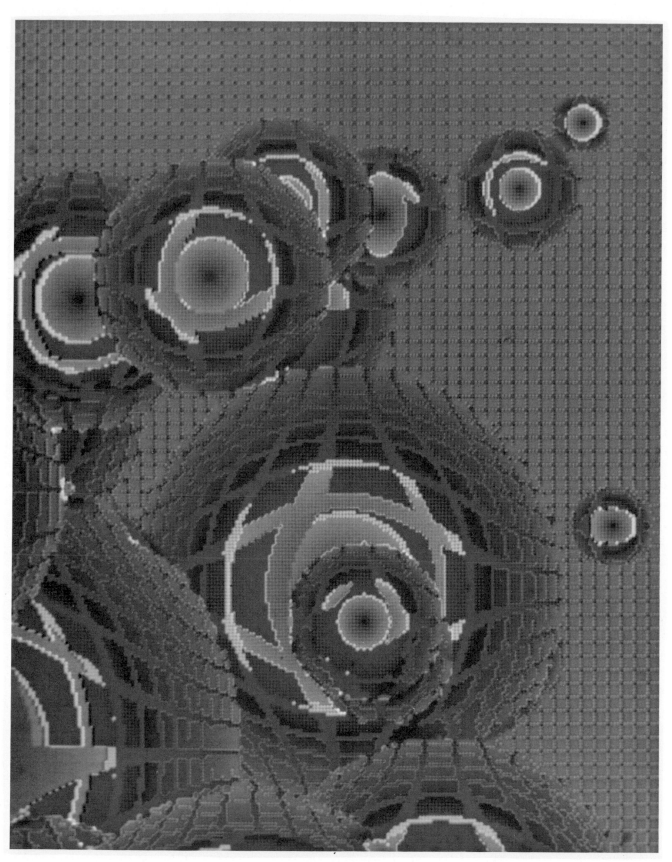

A computer painting, September, 1975.

sketchy, rather vague, set of goals whereas the scientist has a well-defined set. An artist starts out with a tentative plan and then feels around until he finds something he likes. The end result may not even resemble what he started out to achieve. There are, of course, grey levels in this black-and-white description—especially in the area of the more creative programmers and artists; but, then again, it is the creative individual who can overcome rigid processes and change his thinking to fit the situation.

When our stereotyped programmer gets an error or unexpected result he straightens out his program to give the 'right' result, but when our stereotyped artist gets an error or unexpected result he evaluates it from an esthetic viewpoint and may incorporate it into his work or allow it to dictate the direction of the work if it 'feels good.' The former philosophy is more authoritarian—greater emphasis is placed on rules—generating and obeying them. The artist likes to break rules if he can. He wants to disprove the seemingly absolute.

The difference in methodology, incidentally, makes it difficult for the artist to write a definite proposal to get funds for the creation of a computer art environment. It is difficult for him to outline goals, needs, and step-by-step procedures in a well-defined scientific manner when his work is not based on these methods.

Now a major problem with achieving access to a flexible computer art medium is the initial cost of setting it up: $50,000 for a computer, $80,000 for a frame-buffer, $5,000 for a tablet, and $5,000 for a color TV monitor. This means that none but the wealthiest artists can afford his own electronic 'paints-and-brushes.' However, as the cost of everything else is on its way up, the cost of computer equipment is plummetting downward. In five years the cost of this equipment should be within the range of an art department budget.

Let us assume that the artist has secured use of this hardware, has developed some software, and has generated some images on the TV monitor. What are the possibilities of him freeing his images from the electronic cage and putting them into some form which he can hold in his hands? Right now all he can do is record the image on photographic paper or film. Putting it on video tape—another possibility—is just the transferral of his images from one electronic cage to another. Both methods involve transferring to a medium other than the one with which the artist is working. This may be more palatable if one makes the analogy with the etching medium—where the artist works on a metal plate and prints his images onto paper. Or one could take solace in the realization that most art is seen through art magazines where the art magazine reader has left to his imagination the sizes, true colors, and the textures of paintings. Actually, a numerical bridge can be constructed in the transferral of images from the TV monitor to film so that the light intensities are adjusted to make the film image match as closely as possible the TV image.

If the artist does not like the above input-output devices, the versatility of this medium is its ability to handle quite varying devices for input or output. All that is required is that each device have a wire or two containing electrical current which varies within a certain prescribed range. The rest is within the imagination of the individual designing the device.

If one considers the question as to which medium is preferable—the computer or paint-and-canvas, the answer ultimately lies with the individual. Exciting works or boring works can be produced in either medium.

Salt Lake City, Utah
August 1975

BIBLIOGRAPHY

Gilot, Francoise, and Lake, Carlton. *Life With Picasso*. New York, N.Y.: The New American Library, Inc., 1965.

Lebel, Robert. *Marcel Duchamp*. New York, N.Y.: Grossman Publishers, 1959.

KEN KNOWLTON

The computer does not make it possible to define or execute complex processes—this possibility exists independently—but the computer does make execution fast enough to be done interactively with further human decisions, accurate enough to avoid mistakes, and cheap enough to afford a great deal of experimentation. Whether the computer is defining a new branch of art is an open and difficult question, particularly in the area of works defined entirely by logic (i.e., those resulting from processes with no natural input or human interaction once the computer program has been written). This latter category, the most severe form of 'computer' art, I would like to discuss, beginning with a definition of art.

What is art?

The process of doing or making art is a particular kind of giving or offering. If I give you something that is not obviously related to your physical or psychological well-being—not food or protection or direct affirmation or sex—and if it is a concoction of my own design and construction, then it is some sort of symbolic gift. If furthermore it is a new symbol, without a previously agreed upon referent or meaning, I am probably trying to present something that verges on being unpresentable by communication protocols established to date. This symbolic presentation, where the symbols themselves have no clearly defined meanings or usage, I shall take to be the usual (at least my) definition of 'art.'

A work of art furthermore has a purpose and a function. The artist usually intends it to be an augmentation of the viewer's experience: it may either be a new and interesting or useful experience in itself and/or it is a clue or suggestion for reorganization of past and present experience, or a guide to organization of future experience. This sort of communication requires not agreement on meanings (the usual prerequisite of communication) but only an understanding that the artist is offering something to at least one receptive person. The recipient's inferred meanings and use of the work may be more, or less, or deviant from, the giver's intent or hope; the recipient may or may not in addition be able to experience vicariously in hindsight the experience of the artist.

As with other gifts, the psychological function is clearly different for giver and receiver. For the artist, the function is that of producing, being vital and effective, of creating,

generating, and by this sort of catharsis, washing out the products of this effort by actually constructing, dispersing, and dispensing. "It is more blessed to give than receive" in this context means that the experience of having been a channel of flow and processing of ideas and things, that come from somewhere and go to somewhere, is usually the more soothing reward. (It is also nice if people acknowledge, appreciate, or even acclaim, but for people whose mommies loved them this is of secondary importance.) The function of art for the recipient is more diffuse, more difficult to discern or deduce: art is an agitation which causes his/her experience to be enlarged in one or more of many possible ways.

The Role of Tools

Works of art are produced by the use of tools and materials: brushes and paint, hammers and chisels and stone, torches and slabs of metal. Some sets of tools are more complicated in function and use, and in some cases the end product exhibits a corresponding or resultant complexity.

By watching a painter, but not the painting in progress, I can get some idea—but not too much—of the sort of work being produced; conversely, by looking at the finished work I can infer something at least about the overt activity involved in its construction. By watching an author at a typewriter, but not the paper typed on, I need a sharp eye, a quick mind, and a good memory to discern something about what sort of novel is being written. With program-defined computer art, the situation is hopeless: by watching the programmer work, I can scarcely begin to anticipate the nature of the result—I may not even be able to guess whether sounds or pictures are the goal.

Designs from an Explicit Pattern, copyright 1970. Bell Telephone
Laboratories, Inc.

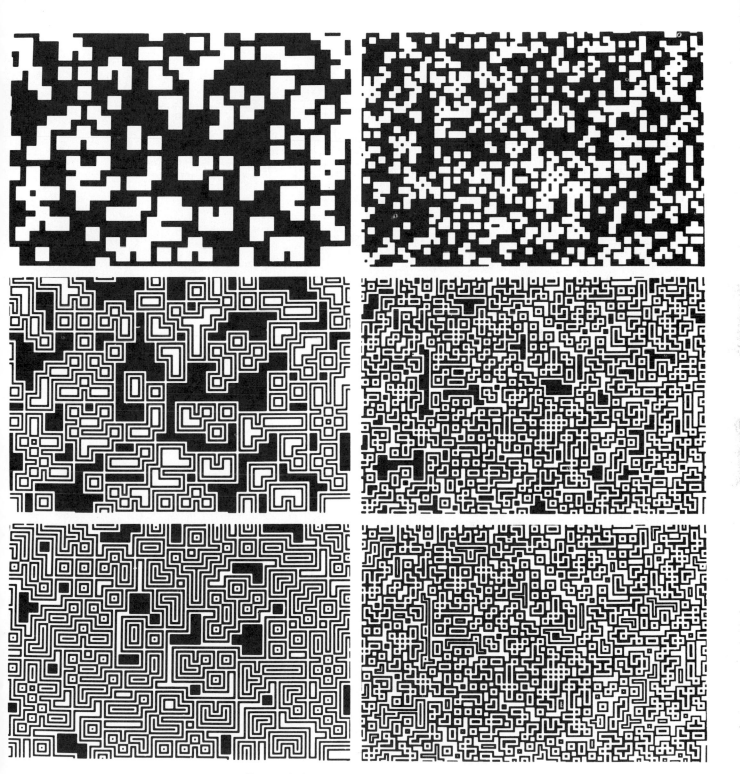

Contours inside and outside scattered boxes.
copyright 1970. Bell Telephone Laboratories, Inc.

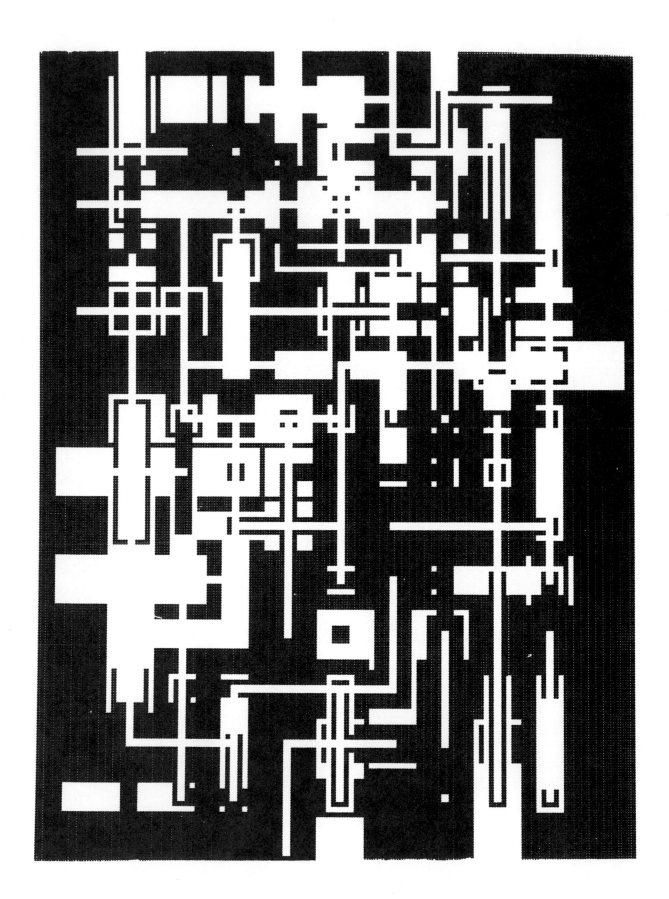

It is the degree of remoteness between the inspiration and the product which I think characterizes computer art more than other kinds: the long and devious way that thoughts and feelings and purposes map into human actions, the way that these actions rigorously define mechanical procedures, and the complicated way in which these in turn produce the result. (Even in an interactive system where an artist uses a 'new sort of paintbrush' in an apparently direct and obvious way, the nature of the resulting art is determined largely by the programs which essentially define a new medium—these programs consist of a complex set of processes that have been selected, carefully or not, from a vast reservoir of potential processes and combinations, and sequences of them.)

The remoteness of thought-to-result is also felt in reverse: it may be extraordinarily difficult to look at a result and recreate anything like either the artist's experience or the machine's process. Sometimes it helps to see a number of results: from them, the viewer can begin to define by induction the parameters of the space of possibilities.

The Nature of the Gift

What sort of enterprise or endeavor is it, then, for the person who programs and produces 'computer art'? Very much the same as with other artists, he/she conceives a process and/or an ultimate product and then proceeds to construct the process which in turn constructs the work. With the computer as the tool, it is usually the intrigue of

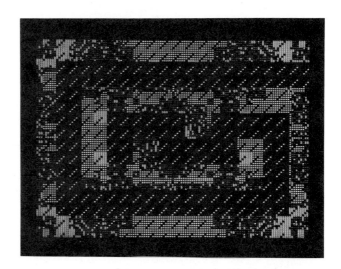

new combinations, sequences, probabilities, relationships, geometries, and logic which fire the imagination in the definition of new processes; it is the complexities and austerities, made easily possible by the machine, and the sharpness, smoothness or coarseness of the imagined result which stir a sense of anticipation.

But to the viewer, what sort of a gift or offering can a computer-generated work be taken to be? Not only are the symbols new and ambiguous as with other art; they seem, still at this stage, to be new *kinds* of symbols. They may in themselves *be* a new experience—sometimes very delightful in ways difficult to achieve 'by hand.' But they don't readily relate to other experiences. There is an uneasy suggestion that a new kind of symbolism is trying to emerge, but what the symbolic meanings might be taken to be remains incredibly nebulous. One can scarcely begin to infer the syntax, much less the semantics.

We seem to have here something like a bridge to be gapped or a gap to be bridged—I'm not surprised that different people have different answers to that. I prefer to think of it as a drawbridge: sometimes down so that we can apply our complete set of contemporary abilities to our total set of current needs—sometimes up to protect ourselves from the precisions and rigidities which the machines, and to some extent their users, must necessarily follow.

Plainfield, New Jersey
January 1976

JOSEPH SCALA

As early in my life as I can remember I wanted to create art and be an artist. Most of my pre-school time was spent drawing and making things, collecting junk for no other reason than I liked the color or the shape. Elementary school was standard city public education with its multi-diversions and cueing regimentation. But the desire and the artistic production did not wane. City high school was a mixture of excitement, encouragement and fear. Gang fights were the order of the day and walking into the gym locker room to find someone sprawled out on the floor with a bloody broken nose was not very unusual; it didn't even make the school paper. Then we moved to the suburbs with the 'good' school. In the 'good' school there weren't any gang fights—just mischievous teenagers who if they happened to be on a school team had their egos blown by the coaches to the point where they thought they could do anything and get away with it and they usually did. This was the 'good' school. Reading, writing, arithmetic and football, not necessarily in that order, is what makes boys into men and the girls—well, the girls were supposed to get the right man and not worry about anything else. So in the 'good' school one took math, physics, chemistry, football and if you couldn't make it, they put you in art. Naturally, I took the important courses because I knew what was necessary to be a man.

Art school? Do you want to be a bum? Are you prepared for art school? —you don't have a portfolio! Study chemistry—chemists make big money. One year of chemistry from 8 a.m. to 6 p.m. in a technical trade college and then a transfer to a liberal arts college. My first art course in college was an art history course taught by Jules Olitsky. His opening remark was "Does anyone want to buy a painting for a few hundred dollars?" The class laughed! "Professor Olitsky, I'd like to show you my work." "I believe you've got something, Scala. Keep working." God damn! Somebody wants me to make art! Tuition has to be paid—nobody is going to support three years of art—major, study mathematics, take art on the side. Graduated with a B.S. in math—now what? Get a job, get married, have a child and make art.

The job: first engineering aide in a large defense plant, thought about using the defense plant facilities to make

'Exploring II', 40½ H. x 52¼ W. inches. PDP-10 computer, EXPLOR system,
line printer, enlarged by program and painted on with acrylic paint.

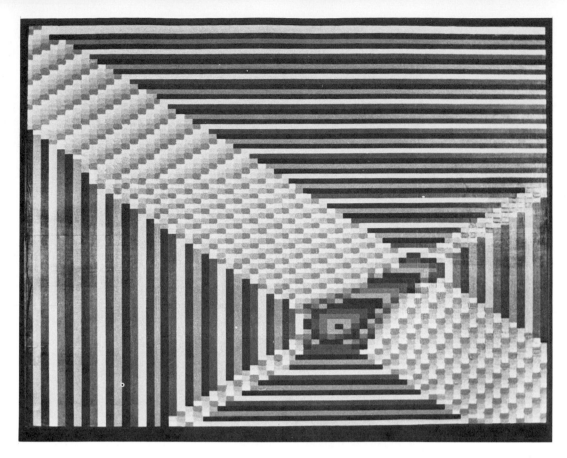

'Exploring I', 40½ H. x 52¼ W. inches. PDP-10 computer, EXPLOR system,
line printer, enlarged by program and painted on with acrylic paint.

art. Nine months employment, promise of promotion to assistant engineer within several additional months, I resigned! — couldn't stand it. Three months of travel in Europe returning home penniless, carless and jobless. Now mathematics teacher in secondary school.

The art: where is my head? I'm thinking equations and technology all day ... why not combine those ideas in the art? This is where I left traditional art and started making kinetic art. Moving sculpture that generated virtual volumes and incorporated time as a fourth dimension. This brought some success, a few sales and some important exhibitions. Decision time—to continue teaching full time in secondary school and making art nights, weekends and during vacations; go to graduate school for an MFA and try to get a college teaching job; or just stop gainful employment and make art. I chose to go to graduate school and there is where I was first introduced to the computer. I took a course in computer graphics for architects and made my first cal-comp drawing. The second drawing I tried on my own was a little disappointing. I got the x and y coordinates mixed up and my output was a large black mess centered in the middle of the page. At that point I decided that the computer was not ready for the artist and I went back to making interactive sculpture. After graduating from Cornell I got a teaching position in the Department of Experimental Studios at Syracuse University. In collaboration with an engineering colleague I designed and implemented a new course in art-engineering which included topics such as mechanics, light, electronics, and their aesthetic applications. Searching for contemporary technology to apply to art I took a workshop in computer-graphics from Dr. Ken Knowlton and using his EXPLOR software system, which he designed for artists, a new world opened up to me. EXPLOR offered me a system that could be understood visually and enabled

me to learn Fortran by applying the Fortran language to the solution of graphic problems as opposed to the traditional mathematical approach. This I believed would be the best way to teach art students and artists how to program in Fortran and make graphic art at the same time. I immediately acquired the EXPLOR system and brought it back to Syracuse University and proceeded to set up and offer a course in computer-graphics especially for art students. It worked! Within a few weeks art students who had never seen a computer and who had little or no mathematical training were writing programs in Fortran and producing graphic images.

The EXPLOR images are painted on a high speed line printer making the time between execution and finished print extremely fast. In fact, with our DEC-writer terminals the image is typed back almost immediately. This is a tremendous advantage for the artist because he/she can see the results and make changes in a more or less interactive continuous way. My students came from a number of different disciplines which made the total class output tremendously varied. Printmakers photographed their computer output, made kodaliths and used the kodaliths to produce photo-silkscreens, photo-lithos, photo-etchings and embossings. Weavers used their designs to produce needle points, tapestries and rugs. Others painted on the computer prints, drew on them, colored them with various mediums and made collages. Still others made animated films and video tapes. With the assistance of the Syracuse University computing center and a talented computer specialist named David Carr, we were able to get the EXPLOR system outputted on our VB10-C display. The display is a cathode ray tube which looks like a T.V. and can produce the programmed images as points of light on the screen. The images can then be sequenced so that they can be filmed a single frame at a time to make an animated movie. This capability led to an interdisciplinary course which was put together between my wife, Patsy Scala, who is an expert in video art and television, a colleague from the film department and myself. We were able to successfully integrate all three art forms and produce color films and color video tapes of unusual design and effect. We offer this course at Syracuse University during the summer. The computer-art program in the Department of Experimental Studios now includes a number of different software systems which can be outputted on the line-printer, the DECwriter terminals, the VB10-C display and the cal-comp plotter. One system presently being implemented can be used to design 3-d sculpture, another can write poetry and yet another created by Ruth and Jay Leavitt can stretch patterns into different shapes.

In my own work I have used the computer to generate animated sequences which have been transferred from film to video and back to film in collaboration with my wife. At the present time my greatest interest has been in generating two-dimensional graphic images and allowing random elements to integrate my basic pattern with

elements that artists would be concerned with; namely, sensitivity of the line, texture, variety of available paper, size, color, ease of execution and natural interaction. It seems reasonable and to a limited extent it is happening that as more artists start using the computer the hardware and software will be modified for the artists' needs. And as the price of computers continue to drop the computer will become a standard studio tool. If not for every artist personally then collectively through centers designated for the exclusive production of computer art.

The impact that the computer will have on art as a whole will be greater than the impact the camera had on the visual arts. Kids are coming out of elementary school knowing how to type and use electronic calculators, if not computers, and to them using a computer to make art will seem as natural and obvious as artists who now use a pencil. Naturally not all artists will use computers but their work will be influenced by the computer and I believe will tend to go toward heavily textured surfaces incorporating different physical materials and be multi-dimensional in size and medium. The computer will also have a tremendous effect on the film making industry by

'Exploring III', 40½ H. x 52½ W. inches. PDP-10 computer, EXPLOR system, line printer, enlarged by program and painted on with acrylic paint.

preset limits of minimum and maximum dimensions. The random factor is of interest to me because it gives the computer a limited decision-making capability in my design which is similar to the controlled randomness that Pollock achieved in dripping paint on to a canvas. My problem has been that where computer images seem to integrate naturally into film and video the hardcopy output often has an artificial machine look. For this reason I have found it necessary to bring my hand onto the final result through painting and drawing. I have generated line-printer designs using the EXPLOR software system with multi-colored ribbons. As far as I know I was the first artist to use different colored line printer ribbons to make original works of computer art. The results of this technique are interesting but I still feel the need to work in black and white and combine that with other techniques and mediums to bring my final work into a more traditional aesthetic plane.

The artist has moved in on a system which was originally designed for the military, scientific and business communities. The available hardware was designed for efficiency and speed of output and did not take into account

becoming the standard device for special effects, as well as in abstract video art and animation. Environmental artists will design around and with the computer. In addition I believe the use of the computer to make art has had a startling effect on the computer technologist. Aesthetics has become a major parameter in the technical decision-making process and as more artists become technologically oriented and more scientists become aesthetically aware the future may bring us back to a true union of art and science and the genius of a Da Vinci.

The computer is definitely a tool for the production of art but it is more than just a tool. It is a new way of communicating between persons and the technological environment. The computer is the electronic interface between human thought and aesthetic expression which will allow human kind to tap and communicate those cords of humanity necessary for the continuation of human existence with and in our scientific-technological culture.

Syracuse, New York
October 1975

KAREN E. HUFF

COMPUTER WEAVING: MODERN TECHNOLOGY CONFRONTS AN ANCIENT CRAFT*

As both a handweaver and a computer scientist, I am always interested in ways to apply the power of the computer to the study of weaving. So, when I had an opportunity to experiment with the capabilities of a plotter, I saw a chance to study textile structure through diagrams drawn by computer. Other computer applications in weaving have been pursued[1],[2], but none had attempted to exploit the potential of the plotter as the primary visual output device.

Mention of plotters almost automatically raises visions of graphs, maps, and 3-D perspective views. Because these are the typical uses of a plotter, these are also the applications for which support packages have been developed to make the plotter more accessible. But this accessibility tends to channel potential plotter use along these already well-traveled paths.

What is obscured is the fact that a plotter is a general purpose line-drawing device. After all, everything it can do is accomplished with two primitive functions, drawing a straight line and moving to a new position without drawing. The weaving application I had in mind might demonstrate the usefulness of the plotter in a non-traditional role. With a big smile, I told my colleagues at the Kansas State University Computing Center that I was going to "teach the computer to weave."

Historical Loom-Computer Connection

That computers should now be used in textile applications merely brings full circle the historical connection between looms and computers. Charles Babbage (1792-1871) conceived the idea of a general-purpose, programmable computer around 1833, attributing his inspiration directly to the Jacquard loom.[3] The pattern woven by a Jacquard loom (invented in 1805) is controlled by a string of pasteboard cards laced together and processed sequentially, with the woven pattern determined by the arrangement of holes punched in the cards. Here is the origin of the punched card concept!

With the Jacquard loom in mind, Babbage envisioned a computer with a string of program cards directing sequential arithmetic operations according to punched holes and a string of data cards specifying the operands of the calculations. Babbage realized that the Jacquard card system could be used to store coded information to achieve the mechanical actions needed to drive his 'Analytical Engine.' As a contemporary commentator wrote, "We may say most aptly, that the Analytical Engine weaves algebraical patterns just as the Jacquard loom weaves flowers and leaves."

Plots of Textile Structure

The inspiration for my experiments was to capitalize on the unique line-drawing capabilities of the plotter to diagram a new representation of textile structure. The traditional graph-paper approach (Figure 1) shows the three essential elements of the weaving instructions—threading, tie-up, and treadling (collectively, the draft)—aligned around the cloth diagram. This cloth diagram shows the exact interlacement of the (vertical) warp

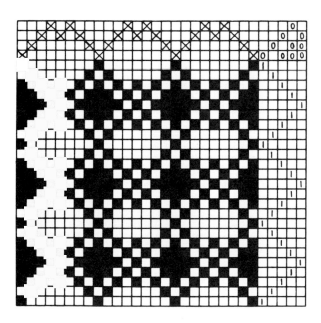

Computer Weaving, figure 1: standard drafting system showing three repeats of Waffle Weave.

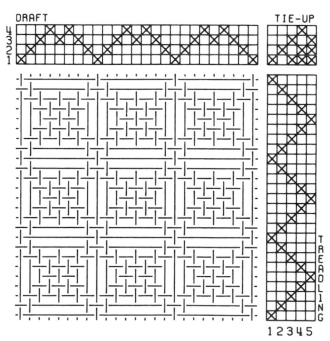

Computer Weaving, figure 2: computer-generated diagram; compare to figure 1.

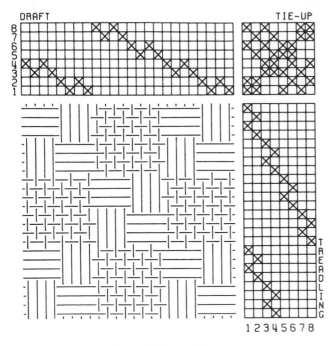

figure 3: 'M's and O's'

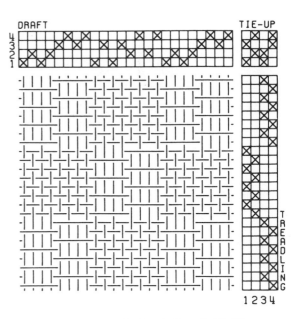

figure 4: 'Apparel Yardage in Extended Twill'.

threads with the (horizontal) weft threads. Each warp-weft crossing is represented by a square on the graph paper, white if weft crosses over warp, black if warp crosses over weft. While this representation shows the design clearly, it doesn't look very much like fabric.

What if, instead, the cloth diagram were to use lines to represent the individual warp and weft threads, with breaks showing where some threads cross under others? Such lines, if drawn with a broad point pen, might look much more like the threads of actual fabric magnified for study purposes. Would such a representation, with its totally different appearance, shed more light on the nature of weaving structure and how that structure can best be exploited in the design process? That was the central question for my experiments.

Weaving Structure Fundamentals

In order to be able to write a computer program to plot such a textile illustration, I had to be thoroughly familiar with the basics of weaving structure myself. So I reviewed these fundamentals. The essence of structure reduces to a pattern of warp and weft crossings—where does the warp cross over the weft, and where does it cross under?

Handweavers can look at fabric structure from one of two points of view. Given a complete draft, a weaver will want to know what the structural appearance of the woven fabric will be like. This question is answered by writing down the threading, tie-up, and treadling on graph paper and working out the cloth diagram. Weavers find this fairly straightforward, since it amounts to imitating the actions of the loom as successive groups of warp threads are raised so that the weft thread may pass under in its back-and-forth course.

On the other hand, it is not uncommon for a weaver to admire a piece of fabric, handwoven or not, and want to know how it could be woven. In this case, there is only the cloth diagram represented by the finished fabric itself; this must be copied onto graph paper, and then the threading, tie-up, and treadling can be generated from it. Without the natural parallels to the physical process of weaving, this task is rather abstract and therefore rather more tedious.

In both cases, there is a simple repetitive procedure to follow in generating the missing element from the information at hand.[4] This skill of 'weaving on paper' should be in every handweaver's repertoire, and this skill was exactly what I wished to embody in a computer program which would plot textile structure. 'Weaving on paper' has all the negative attributes of a rote hand operation—it is tedious, time-consuming, and prone to error. Therefore I expected a bonus for transferring it to an automatic computer operation, a bonus in accuracy and ease-of-use.

Computer Implementation

Because all the weaving data fits so naturally into two-dimensional array form, designing and writing the program was straightforward. By taking advantage of the language features in PL/1, I was able to design an input form easy for weavers (or naive computer users) to work with. Almost all of the plotting was accomplished with the two plotting primitives; the only other plotting function used was the one which plots text annotations. Because so few plotting support routines were needed, it made sense to enjoy the use of PL/1 and fake the expected Fortran calling protocol as needed. The program was developed on an IBM 370/158 using a CalComp 663 drum plotter.

With this versatile tool for textile studies at my fingertips, I selected a variety of drafts with which to experiment, to see what could be learned about structure from the computer-generated illustrations. With the computer assuming responsibility for the tedious part of the processing, I found that in very little time I had generated many illustrations to study. Some examples are given in Figures 2-4.

Insights From Computer Diagrams

At first, I was disappointed that the computer diagrams did not have the striking impact of the traditional representation. This can be seen by comparing Figures 1 and 2, which are both of the same draft. I soon realized, however, that the reason for this lies in the built-in color bias of the traditional form. The cloth diagram on graph paper actually shows a white weft and a black warp, whereas both warp and weft are black in the computer version.

Here is clear evidence of the key role played by color in enhancing or suppressing the visual design possibilities of a given draft. Because the color bias is removed, the

figure 5: 'Cat Tracks'.

figure 6: 'Summer and Winter'.

TREADLING

1234

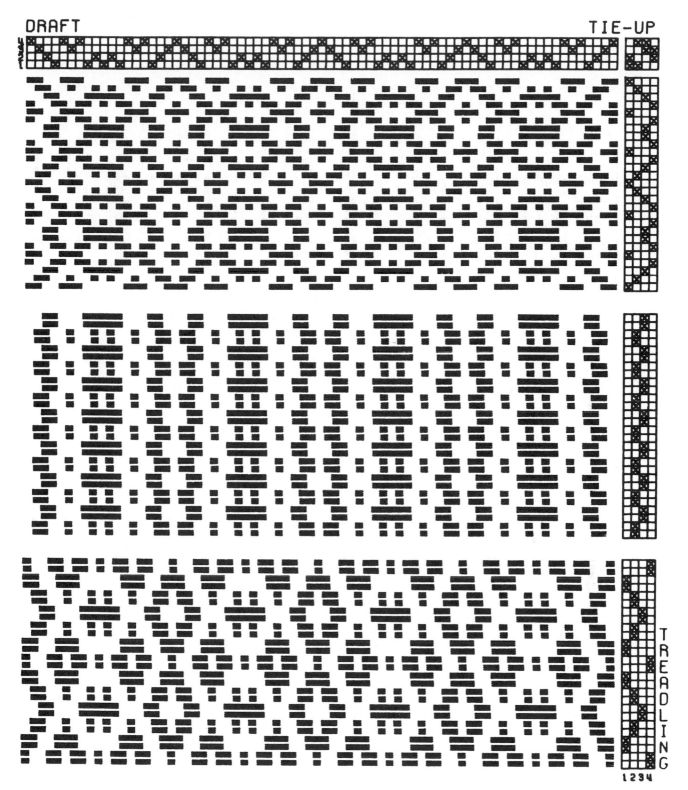

figure 7: 'Weaver's Fancy'.

computer diagram is a more pure representation of fabric structure alone. Designing color schemes based on these diagrams is free of any predisposition toward built-in color properties.

I next found that the representation used in the computer illustrations actually encouraged me to examine the structure on a very detailed level, for example, by following the paths of individual threads. I saw new ways and means of tailoring yarn and color selections to a specific draft. In figure 2, for example, the warp threads on harnesses 1 and 2 follow a path of long skips; they are prominent in the structure. To take advantage of this, a fancy yarn could be threaded there to emphasize its decorative value; or, a certain color of yarn could be threaded there to emphasize its color value. These insights are due to the more realistic thread representation used in the computer diagrams.

As it happened, some of my computer illustrations were of drafts for which I had pictures of finished woven fabric. By comparing the illustrations with the pictures, the importance of what happens to fabric after it is removed from the loom was made very clear. For many weaves, the characteristic texture will develop only after the loom tension is removed and the yarns are allowed to relax into their new positions. Even simple plain weave "softens" in appearance as well as texture after removal from the loom; this softening is completed by the first washing of the fabric.

By studying the computer illustrations, this kind of softening of contours in the weave can be predicted. Areas of close thread interlacement will draw together proportionately more than areas of loose interlacement. For example, again in Figure 2, the 3-dimensional "waffle" characteristic of this weave will develop as the plain weave areas draw in together, further emphasizing the long skips in the areas of looser interlacement.

In an illustration showing many design repeats, these differing design areas can be readily recognized and their interrelationships examined. While it is tedious to diagram many repeats by hand, the computer program can diagram many as easily as one, thereby encouraging this kind of study.

Design Implications

As I studied the computer diagrams, I found myself looking at the weaving design process from a new perspective. My experiments showed me that structure is in itself a separate and crucial design element, one of three along with yarn and color. Each element must complement the others for the total design to be effective; the structure, yarns, and colors must all work together, whether each assumes a major or subordinate role.

The elements of yarn and color are shared by all the fiber arts—weaving as well as knitting, crocheting, knotting, twining, and braiding. The structural characteristics distinguish any one from any of the others. Anni Albers has suggested that the historical supremacy of weaving over the other fiber arts was due to the ease with which weaving structure lent itself to mechanization.[5]

Further Developments

Because the program was so convenient to use, I continued to make plots regularly to help with my own design work. I often went down to the machine room to watch the plots in progress, and seeing the partially finished plots suggested further developments which might be attempted. An interesting effect was created when only the weft threads had been plotted, and the warp not yet laid across it. What if some program options were added so that only the weft would be plotted, and that plotted very heavily? Would this approach simulate the design appearance of weaving systems, such as colonial overshot, where a dark weft forms a pattern against a light background warp?

For such systems, there are traditional ways of weaving which give a standard structure and texture; the design problem for these systems is one of creating and/or adjusting a pattern to pleasing proportions. Although the emphasis would be entirely opposite to what I had already done (concentrating on color differences rather than removing them), I could pursue this new approach with minor extensions to the existing program.

A most interesting problem arose while making these extensions. The program required considerable adjustment to give the desired visual effect. When the weft lines were too long or too thin, the pattern was lost in a jumble— even though I knew what pattern to look for, my eye could not resurrect it. As I tuned the plotting by shortening and widening the lines, the pattern emerged, at first tentatively and finally with great clarity. In fact, for sheer drama, it would be hard to improve on the new plot style.

Once the plotting was in adjustment, I quickly generated diagrams in several systems. Colonial overshot, which is of considerable historic importance, is represented in Figure 5. When selecting such a draft, the weaver needs to know which part of the draft corresponds to which part of the pattern motif; or, the weaver wants to coordinate a pattern with a border motif, and needs to know how the two will fit together. The new style of plots meets these needs. Figure 5 also shows the optical illusion quality found in many overshot patterns, and can be viewed as an interesting design independent of a weaving interpretation.

A system such as summer and winter has several classic textures, all slight treadling variations of the same basic threading. In order to understand the differences between them, they can be plotted and compared as in Figure 6. Then there are basic threadings which have virtually limitless variations with a large range of potential patterns. Instead of weaving samples of these pattern variations, it is possible to plot samplers showing the many possibilities. Such a sampler for Weaver's Fancy is shown in Figure 7.

With the addition of this new feature, the program has become quite a versatile learning and design tool. The value of computer weaving lies both in the automatic nature of the program as well as in the visually meaningful diagrams possible via the plotter. This creates for the designer-weaver an opportunity rich for exploration where creative energies may be concentrated in creative experimentation. Charles Babbage would no doubt be pleased to see that modern computers are repaying the long-standing debt they owe to weaving in the currency of applications such as this.

Manhattan, Kansas
September 1975

REFERENCES

1. Lourie, Janice. *Textile Graphics/Computer-Aided.* New York: Fairchild Publications, 1973.
2. Velderman, Pat. "Computer Generated Overshot Variations." *Handweaver and Craftsman.* Fall, 1971. Pgs. 10-11.
3. Babbage, Charles. *Charles Babbage and His Calculating Engines.* Ed. Philip and Emily Morrison. New York: Dover, 1961.
4. Frey, Berta. *Designing and Drafting for Handweavers.* New York: Macmillan Company, 1958. Chapts. 1-2.
5. Albers, Anni. *On Weaving.* Middletown, Connecticut: Wesleyan University Press, 1965.

MILJENENKO HORVAT

I have no particular theory or philosophy about my work. I try to do what I like and what I am able to do—technically speaking. So I will just try to answer your questions as sincerely as I can.

"How/why did you become involved with the computer (in producing art)?"

It was available—or almost—so I tried it and liked it.

"What is your art background?"

I am a painter since mid-fifties.

"What role does the computer play for you ... simulation, tool, etc.? What is your role?"

Extremely fast executing tool.

"Are your computer works related to non-computer art?"

It's not related or very slightly.

"Do you have a final image in mind when work begins?"

Yes, but not always a very clear one.

"Could your work be done without the aid of a computer? If yes, why use the computer?"

Of course it could be done without a computer. But to produce the same amount of work, it would take a couple of thousand times more in time and energy than I can afford.

"To what extent are you involved in the technical production of your work, for example, in programming?"

I work closely with Serge Poulard, an excellent programmer.

"Do you feel art work created with a computer has now or will have an impact on art as a whole in the future?"

It has very little impact now on art as a whole; I hope the impact will grow in the future.

"Do you intend to continue using the computer to create art pieces?"

Yes.

"Do you recommend the use of the computer for others in creating works of art?"

Yes, but only if the use of the computer is justified by creative needs or sensibility of a particular artist.

Montreal, Canada
October 1975

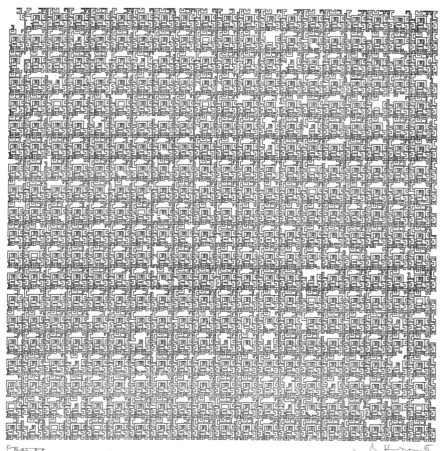

'ERATOS', electrostatic point printer drawing.

JOHN WHITNEY

COMPUTATIONAL PERIODICS

We may assume that a time will come when that which I am about to describe will name itself—but for now: 'Computational periodics' is a propositional and tentative term which may help to designate a new unified field for a heterodimensional art; a field whose special dimension is time. An art which is temporal, as music itself; being, that is, spatio-temporal. An art whose time has come because of computer technology and an art which could not exist before the computer. Even though this art will be found in the notebooks of Leonardo and has been in the collective imagination, like the flying-machine, since his epoch it was a technological impossibility until the development of computer graphics.

Rhythm, meter, frequency, tonality and intensity are the periodic parameters of music. There is a similar group of parameters that set forth a picture domain as valid and fertile as the counterpoised domain of sound. This visual domain is defined by parameters which are also periodic. 'Computational periodics' then is a new term which is needed to identify and distinguish this multidimensional art for eye and ear that resides exclusively within computer technology. For notwithstanding man's historic efforts to bridge the two worlds of music and art through dance and theatre, the computer is his first instrument that can integrate and manipulate image and sound in a way that is as valid for visual, as it is for aural, perception.

That rare talent of the composer to create music which is self sustaining, i.e., the power of music to capture and hold our attention, is a sophisticated and subtle art which has been the exclusive gift of only a few composers in each of many past generations. It was a pedagogic skill, however, that a pupil might learn, provided he was himself possessed with latent genius. In this century all that pedagogy has been reduced to anxious uncertainty. The harmonic and metric traditions, for one thing, seem to be untranslatable into the new periodic resources that abound in computer technology. The body of knowledge that resulted, by the nineteenth century, in musical works of ponderous scale and proportion, is a lost art. By the standards of the Baroque era the present has retrogressed to infantilism.

The new composer, and the visual artist who may aspire to deal with teleonomic structures, could as well be the child of some early dark age. The Twentieth Century began with technology and has reaped a whirlwind of cultural dislocations and amnesia. Materials and forms and attitudes are so altered that past traditions are generally moribund.

Also from the point of view that this Century is but an episode in the life of human culture, it is clear that more paraphernalia of this epoch may be castoff than will survive into the next. Yet surely the computer will not. A solid state image storage system will replace the silver chemical ribbon and cinema will eventually be interred in the archival museum. But computer and computer graphics bring to mind the kind of tools that may characterize an age succeeding this century's age of the machine.

The computer is the coequal of the entire repertoire of musical instrumentation and heir to that domain of musical sound. At the same time, the computer is the ultimate kinetic image generative instrument. The kinetic image is in truth the creation of computer graphics since the cine or television camera is but a recording device and the hand-drawn image of motion is but a cartoon of motion.

Tatlin, Rodchenko, Gabo, Moholy-Nagy, Fontana, Duchamp, Kandinsky, Mondrian, Pollock and twice that many more artists of this century testify to the drive toward dynamic organization of energy and force in art. And toward ephemeralization of the art object in painting and sculpture. The past decade has seen that direction lead many artists to cinema, exotic technology and experiments with cybernetics. Yet it has passed generally unnoticed that this preoccupation of the last one hundred years has been toward a *musicalization* of visual art. For the urge to produce abstract architectonic structures that possess fluid transformability in visual space is no less than a grand aspiration toward music's double in the visible world. It is as a preoccupation with art in this exclusive sense that we may use the term computational periodics.

Pacific Palisades, California
November 1975

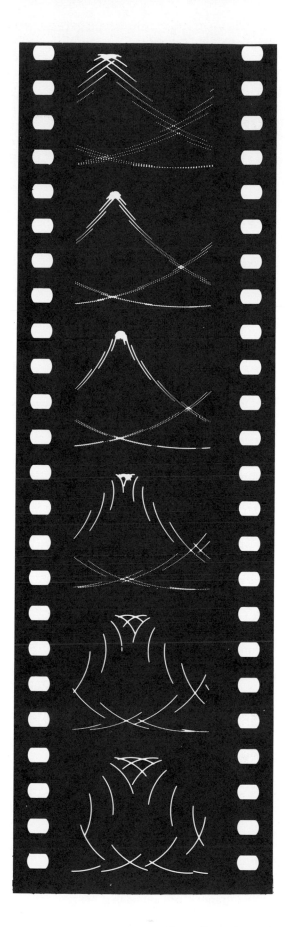 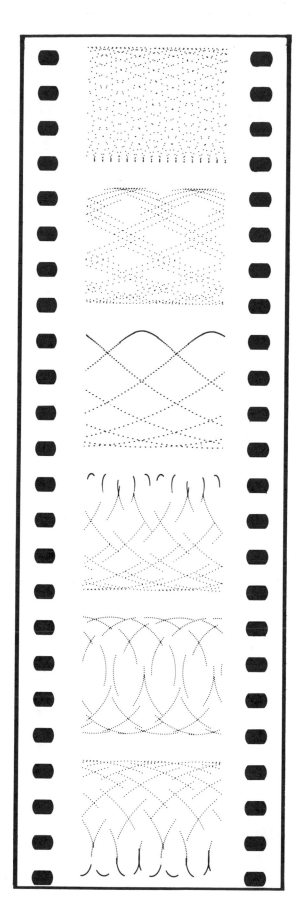

Some diverse harmonic caesura selected from the computer graphics
material used in the film titled 'Arabesque', 1975.

HERBERT W. FRANKE

GRAPHIC MUSIC

The question, what was there before: the idea or the medium, is lively discussed among scientists. The technical medium, is it created only as soon as the idea is there? For its realization is it needed? Or is it the technical know-how from which arises the stimulation of an idea? Practice shows us examples for both cases, where the fundamental rule is of value: the availability of technical knowledge and technical means presents a limiting factor for the realization of ideas. This rule is of value not only for art but also for technology.

A phase picture from the film.

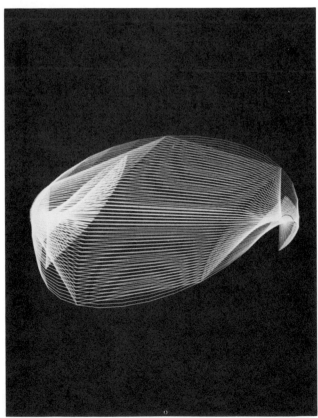

We may conceive of artworks as offers to perception. Every presentation of art must give an opportunity for a conveyance of information. The particularity of aesthetic communication lies in a purposeful preparation of the information-model, an adaption to the ability and readiness for the perceptible reception, and the working up toward the addressee. Therefore it is particularly important that the process of perception succeeds well and continues for a long time.

An inventory of the realm of art, shows us that it is possible to have a distribution of the types of art beyond the sense-channel. Next we have to decide whether the art form is a static or kinetic, temporarily changeable, presentation.

	Heavy-Weight of the Presentation	Static	Kinetic
EYE	Syntactic	Irrelevant Picture	? (Starts in fireworks, water plays, kaleidoscope, etc.)
	Semantic	Graphic Picture	Silent film, pantomime written text
EAR	Syntactic		Music
	Semantic	Static Auditive Presentation	Recitation, radio-play
EYE AND EAR	Syntactic	Not Practicable	Starts in irrelevant animated cartoons and experimental-film, partly ballet
	Semantic		Sound-film, theater, and the like, partly ballet

In this table only the senses seeing and hearing, which are essential for art, are considered. However, there are artlike activities which appeal to other sense-organs, for example the 'art of cooking.' But the spectrum of impressions derivable from cooking is too narrow to produce the abundance and variety of impressions that we expect from a genuine art.

A further point which is very important for art is the distinct effect on the syntactic and semantic planes respectively. It is the distinction between irrelevant models, which impress perhaps with formal or harmonical beauty, and the enciphering of sense capacity. Man is able to set his mind separately upon different planes of structuring, for example on the syntactical and on the semantical one, but understandably the inclination is to occupy himself first with 'sense' statements and the like. Only in subsequent manufacturing phases result the abstracting mental attitude to other order systems anchored in art objects.

In the table a certain spot is marked by a question mark. The point represents the unobjective visual presentation which corresponds to music in the realm of auditive art forms.

This is a good example of how much the lack of technical means may influence cultural developments. While in music there were very early technical mediums for managing sound-effects, the real possibilities lie in the visual realm, but were not realized. The idea of a graphic play of forms, 'Graphic Music' could only be realized since the development of optical-electronic means.

Therefore we ask whether the requirement of such an art form exists. Often it is presumed that the absence of such an artform goes back to the deficiency of this need. But it shows that man possesses an appreciation of forms and colors in dynamic movement. The fascination starting from the observation of waterwaves and flames is a proof of this. But there are also historical examples where there were attempts to create techniques to realize this idea. Examples of this are fireworks, artificial water-plays, perhaps fountains illuminated in colors and the Kaleidoscope. But all these techniques have many faults. For instance it is difficult to control these apparitions. Moreover, they offer a relatively small complexity of perceptual effects. A principle possibility for the realization of 'Graphic Music' was offered first by the trickfilm in its original form, the animated cartoon; practicability is missing. The production of phase pictures is extremely troublesome, taking up much time and is very expensive. This example clearly shows that technical means alone are inadequate; economic feasibility is also required. Another assumption relates to control. The physical and psychological qualities must be performed with a relatively high exactitude where the degree of accuracy is determined by the power of distinction of the sense-organs. It is required that, by means of an Artform, there should be produced the best possible realization if it shall not exhaust itself too quickly. But this is only possible if one bestows a certain complexity to the aesthetical pattern. If you use a graphform, which is very inaccurate and superimposed by chance, this complexity is highly restricted. The possibilities determined by the certain art-form will be reduced unnecessarily; the band-width of the human senses is not utilized. The most favorable conditions are where one can produce elements for constructing aesthetical patterns with high exactitude so that they may be described and reproduced. Then it is possible to build up these elements to greatly varied aggregations.

The best example of this is western harmonic music with its different styles. Music-instruments are nothing else than physical precision-machines which allow us to produce exactly reproducible acoustic effects. Experience shows that small deviations from the elementary frequencies, instruments out of tune, make it very difficult to obtain recordings of high quality, and produce unpleasant experiences with perception.

The first technical instrument which allows us to realize the idea of graphic music is the computer with an annexed graphic delivery gear. Elementary units, for example may be line-elements or tokens arranged in a screen. The first computer-graphic installations offered only very restricted possibilities. They used the same methods as in film making with the only difference being that the production of the phase-pictures was controlled according to a program. The transition allows one to view graphic motion-pictures in real time on the fluorescent screen. Interactive systems allow direct exertion of influence on the produced pictures. Thus it becomes possible to go beyond the projected linear course—as it relates to film and to become a sort of 'Graphic improvisation.' Corresponding to what is usual in music, the field of computer-art was founded, breaking new ground and filling a particular void in the scheme of possible Art-forms.

In this direction there were executed practical experiments, especially by John Whitney and his sons and by Kenneth Knowlton and Lillian Schwartz. In the Siemens Research Laboratory the author had access to an installation which was capable of free graphic improvisation through its interactive system. A program written by Gerhard Geitz, Monika Gonauser, Egon Horbst and Peter Schinner for the projection of rotating geometric figurations was enlarged so that a Groundstructure of harmonical geometric courses grew possible. Through aesthetical exploitation the picture elements are built up successively in regular space-angle intervals leading to wandering superpositions, whose projections execute complicated movements upon the picture plane. This

fundamental course serves so to speak, as raw material for further processing, which now takes place interactively. Angle intervals and rate of change of position may be modified. A choice of large angle-intervals introduces the effect of chance and the diminution of the angle-interval of the heterogyne figures leads back again to a state of original order.

This program offers quiet and harmonical picture influences where the degree of order is still raised by symmetric and counter-running movements. Although from the console only a few parameters may be changed, it

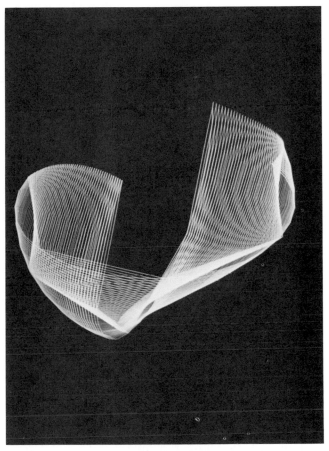

A phase picture from the film.

is still possible to obtain a wide variety of effects. The interspersing of stochastical effects (where the harmony is destroyed) form very drastic phases in the regularity of movement.

Out of our perception-customs we are trained to recognize visual and auditive Information-patterns. The lack of sound in the described courses is felt very negatively on several sides. Conceivably it would be possible to enlarge the program to include auditive effects. However, another possibility was used—musicians freely improvised with simultaneously projected graphical passages. From this two ten-minute Computer films 'Rotations' and 'Projections' were produced. The sound for one film was added during a Computer-Workshop in July 1974, in Bonn where musicians freely improvised with electronic instruments. The sound for the second film was added at the International Musicforum 1974 in Breitenbrunn, Burgenland, Austria. This time some highly qualified free-jazz

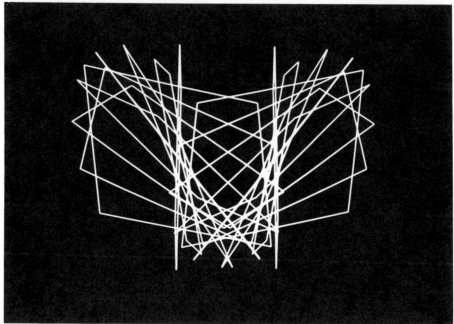

Phase pictures from the films used to create 'Graphic Music'.

musicians participated. Participating in this experiment was a group of ten musicians. During another showing of the film a smaller group took part, among them Karl Berger and Fritz Bauer.

The presentation took place in public, incorporating the audience into the experiment. In the discussion which followed every participant could express his interpretation. Overall the reaction was positive. However, the visual display was difficult for people to relate to. It was too unusual to make value judgments. While our environment confronts us from childhood with musical presentations, we bring along scarcely any knowledge of graphic passages. Evidently, because of this, the natural understanding we have in music is missing, which causes rapid fatigue. The spectator asks for more variety in graphical presentations than he does in acoustical presentation. Such performances of abstract graphic plays should not surpass ten minutes with an uninitiated public. Apart from objections of this sort, the effects on the public were extremely favorable. It shows that graphical music offers the potential to develop into a complex and differentiated form, as is the case with usual music. With film and television we have today at our disposal the optical means of delivery and the practical assumptions for the spreading of new aesthetical forms of presentation. These could grow to a genuine enrichment of our cultural life.

Munich, W. Germany
August 1975

CHARLES CSURI

STATISTICS AS AN INTERACTIVE ART OBJECT

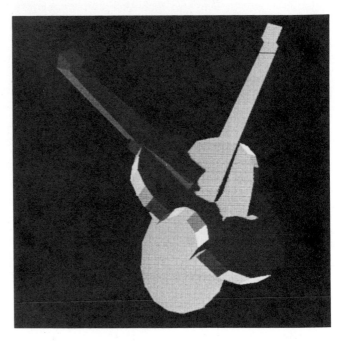

The pictures of the 'apple' and 'violins' (virtual intersection of two musical instruments) illustrate the use of a 3D visible surface algorithm for concave polyhedra.

There are many instances where artists have used the direct analysis of nature (real-world data) to create art. One example is Monet, who worked directly from nature developing relationships of color and light based upon new theories of color. Cezanne's art also epitomized an expression of formal color relationships inspired by external objects or scenes. Artists like Picasso, Duchamp, and later in the mid-1950's and early 1960's, Rauschenberg and Segal used real-world objects in their art. Objects such as a bicycle seat, a chair, an automobile door or a coke machine combined with other materials were used to create a new context for expression. With Kaprow's 'Happenings' one appreciates further extensions of real-world data to include total environments and society as art. The Conceptual Art movement represented other methods and attitudes about objects, abstraction and art—for example, the use of words boldly written on large blueprint paper describing the physical characteristics of a hand; the

words themselves and the blueprint become the art object cuing a mental picture of the hand.

Artists are constantly re-evaluating nature (real-world data) searching for new modes to express some personally felt view of the world and their relationship to it. One might suggest artists utilize real-world data to express a view of reality through the application of transformations to this data.

Data for artistic expression includes the numerical or statistical representation of the external world. As a mass society, we are constantly measuring and evaluating ourselves in order to understand our problems and our needs. We have statistics which are constantly being updated about unemployment, crime, traffic accidents, divorce, mental illness, birth and death, alcoholics, acreage of green space, pollution, longevity .... and many more.

There is a need to understand and solve complex social problems. Through the advent of computer technology, we have developed an enormous capacity to create large data-bases and programs that print out mountains of statistical information. While this capacity is a phenomenal one, we generally have difficulty in knowing how to interpret such data. This data can be extremely complex, especially as one deals with trends, multivariant relationships, dispersion and variation. Many social scientists choose to limit themselves to numeric representations of such data in the belief that this represents a position of neutrality or objectivity. Biderman[1] and a relatively small group of researchers claim that there is a critical need to improve communication and understanding of this information. Improved visual presentation techniques can help us make more rational decisions about how to use resources and solve social problems.

Statistics is a way of making quantitative measurements and looking at reality. Rather than looking to the visual form or the external appearance of reality, the artist can now deal directly with content. It is a new conceptual landscape with its mountains, valleys, flat spaces, dark and light with gradations of texture and color. With computers, the artist can look at statistics representing real-world data about every facet of society—its problems reflecting tragic, comic and even surrealistic viewpoints. The artist has opportunities to express his perceptions of reality in a new way.

Interactive computer graphics offers a mode of interacting with information which is direct, making the numeric representations of data more communicative. The user can interact with mathematical models that simulate social systems or abstract processes or even aesthetic objects. Through computer animation/graphics, the user is given dynamic and pictorial means to view the process of change that is a consequence of his intervention. This enables the user to better understand the complex relationships that produce the results for which his intervention is responsible.

Additional software capabilities provide the user with the ability to modify system parameters through interactive devices and to alter curvilinear relationships without ever having to think of numbers. The simulation model is the same, but its value has been improved by reducing the demands it makes on the user's prior knowledge.

Many of the techniques used in the people-machine communication problems can be applied to computer art and simulations related to aesthetic concerns. Most people are inclined to think of computer art as either static graphics or animated film. In a few instances, physical art objects interfaced to a computer involving sensors reacting to light, sound or heat modify some component in the object establishing a new set of relationships. Another alternative is to view computer art as a real-time object involving user participation and control. The real-time computer art object is an intellectual concept which is made manifest in a visual experience rather than in a finalized material object. This kind of computer art exists only for the time the participant and the computer with a CRT display are interacting as a process. The art object is not the computer or the display, but the activity of both interacting with the participant. In addition to its artistic parameters, the content of this art form is dependent upon the dynamics of a real-time process which gives vitality and life to the visual display through animation and user interaction. Instant visual feedback for the purpose of examining alternatives is another important feature of such objects. Each participant is afforded the opportunity to experience the aesthetic object at a unique level depending upon his background and training.

Real-time computer art systems are designed so that the aesthetic experience is realized for the user through participation. The passive 'viewer' must become an active 'participant' in the actual context provided by the system. A case can be made for the idea that art can alter perception, and that since perception is an active organizing process rather than a passive retention-of-image causation, only by actively participating with the art object can one perceive it—and thus, in perceiving it, change one's reality structure.

A practical illustration of a real-time art object which uses a real-world data base is an interactive system involving animation/graphics and a statistical algorithm. The algorithm was developed into a computer program and a general explanation is offered as background material.

The AID (Automatic Interaction Detector) program was originally developed in 1963 at the University of Michigan. It can potentially be used in any analysis in which one is attempting to explain the variance of the dependent variable as some combination of independent or predictor variables. The program differs from the conventional multiple regression techniques in that no assumptions about the linearity of the model need be made, and that the predictor variables may exhibit many types of interactions without invalidating the analysis.

The AID technique is able to examine the interrelationships of up to 140 predictors. One of the variables is selected as a dependent variable. The technique repeatedly partitions the data into two groups to minimize the error sums of squares of the dependent variable. The output of the program is essentially a tree which summarizes the splitting process which took place. The symmetry or non-symmetry of the resulting tree reflects the interactions of the predictors. The tree may then be plotted on a CRT. A number of user-specified terminating conditions can cause the splitting process to stop. The output of the AID technique is generally presented in reports in the form of trees where each node in a tree represents a set of observations with a particular combination of values in the predictor variables. The mean value of the dependent variable, the number of observations, the predictor values, and the standard deviation is generally included for each node.

The following description of the interactive graphics has been implemented and it is a simulation based upon the AID program. The participant or user is seated in front of the CRT which is interfaced to a computer, and there are interactive devices such as dials, function keys, light pen, joystick, 3-D sonic pen and a keyboard. (The computer is a PDP-11/45 and the graphics display is a Vector General.)

This graphics simulation model starts by growing an AID tree and the user watches for relationships between variables as the tree is created. As is the case with the AID program, there is an order to the growth of the tree. Lower branches of the tree can be deleted if the user desires to reverse this process. One has stored in the computer a simulation of the history (past and projected future) of (real-world data) like key frames in an animation sequence. Through techniques of linear interpolation, smooth and continuous movement through time is achieved. The joystick enables one to control time and by pushing it forward, the user moves forward in time and by pulling it backward, time is reversed. On the CRT, the user has a clock at the lower portion of the screen; a two-dimensional scale is located at the top; and an AID structure is located in the middle. As the user moves the joystick, the structure changes shape and position, the clock moves, for instance, from 1024 to 2048—all of this dynamically in real-time. By pressing a function key and moving the joystick, the user can select a single variable and move it forward or backward through time. The same procedure is used for both linear and shaded pictures. The graphics can dynamically show a critical path development indicating a route to the most important variable in the data; the lines brighten as the path is developed.

Three-dimensional data representation is also used in this model. The tree structures are layered or stacked through the Z axis with each slide representing intervals of time (5 to 10 years) inside a unit cube. A surface is created by connecting lines between slices of time. The front face of the cube represents current time and the surface behind the face shows the history. The user can rotate the three-dimensional model and with the joystick control one can simulate moving through time and the

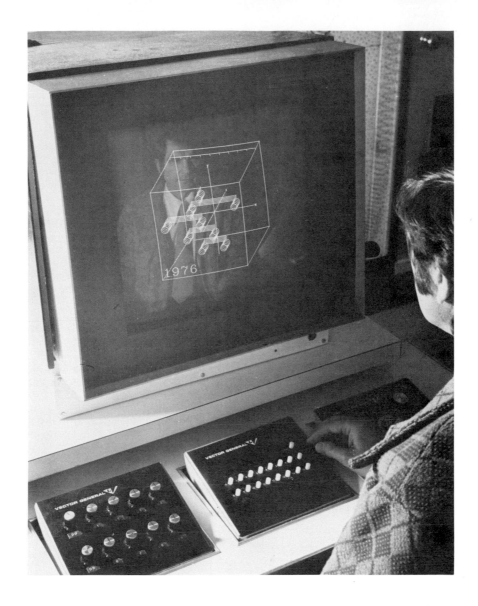

thickness of the layers can symbolize other factors. Then one can rotate the structure to an angle where one can see the top view. This illustrates in more conventional terms, the typical chart with a scale for time along one axis and the percentage of the data along another axis.

While the AID program is represented by a tree structure, some algorithms might use a model of molecular structure. The structure would grow and change color maintaining connectivity with the thickness and color of the connections conveying pertinent information. One could use various geometric objects to represent kinetic models that involve multiple objects and surfaces. Then one could interactively move them through 3-D space and they could change color, shape and size with the speed of movement indicating relationships in the data. Some objects could be represented in a computer program such that they might seem to be made of an elastic material. A function key might indicate some variable to the program. With a 3-D sonic pen and a stereo pair viewing system, one could 'touch' the elastic object and it would dynamically change its shape; using another variable it would change shape differently with the shape itself conveying meaningful data.

The Computer Graphics Research Group at The Ohio State University has as one of its research goals the software development for color video display graphics as a

tool for research scientists. The same hardware and software system could be linked to two-way cable TV. On remote TV sets and terminals, audiences could participate with a statistical art object.

While the original motivation of the visual representation of statistical data (kinostatistics*) is intended to help in the analysis and communication of societal problems, it has great potential as material for artistic expression. Artists have a significant role in the social science aspects of such concerns, but they can also approach real-world data from a purely artistic position to express their views of reality.

Columbus, Ohio
September 1975

ACKNOWLEDGMENTS:

I am especially indebted to the Computer Graphics Research Group for the software and hardware developments which made this experiment possible. Ronald Hackathorn and Allan Myers did the programming for the interactive AID simulation model. George Tressel brought the AID program to my attention and his comments and suggestions are greatly appreciated. The National Science Foundation provided the basic support for the CGRG under grant number DCR 74-00768A01 for the development of real-time animation/graphics techniques as a tool for the research scientist.

*"Kinostatistics for Social Indicators," by Albert D. Biderman, Bureau of Social Research Report, 1971.

CHRISTOPHER WILLIAM TYLER

I was drawn into computer art as a spin-off from experiments in visual perception, which required the production of complex visual stimuli by both analog components and digital computers. This led me to attempt to express some of my amazement at the nervous system in giving rise to the subtleties of perception. The electronic systems that we call computers seemed an interesting way to go about it, and in doing so I discovered a number of viewpoints about the role of computers.

The computer system serves a multiple role as canvas and environment, as tool and creator. The 'canvas' is the range of output devices, from line printer to microfilm plotter, from oscilloscope screen to the control of laser beams. A new medium to work on, with its limitations and idiosyncrasies, has often served to send art on a different tack in the past; so the canvas of computer peripherals might be sufficient to do so again. But computers have vastly more to offer than that.

One of the trends of recent art has been the tendency to operate by selecting from an environment entities that have significance to the artist rather than creating from scratch on a tabula rasa. This approach can be traced back to the Zen potters of China who allowed the glazes to form patterns in the heat of the kiln and then choose particularly fine examples of the result. The same type of selection with minimal control over the medium is the basis for much of photography (but less so in film-making), dadaist art, kinetic art and other approaches, and is I think typical of the use of complex technology. The instruments which are thought of as tools at the disposal of the artist become part of the environment in which the art is produced. The artist selects the output by 'cybernetic serendipity.' The constraints which would be considered limitations in the case of a simple tool such as a brush become a source of inspiration and subject matter in the case of a complex tool like a computer. Although one is accustomed to thinking that anything is possible on a computer, in practice the hardware making up the system, the available programs and cost limitations add up to an adaptive environment which can serve the artist as a continual source of ideas.

The computer can itself act as the creator by the ability to generate random (or pseudorandom) sequences of numbers. On a low level this can operate merely to produce the arrangement of patterns or the selection of

'Morphonome I'.

elements for a design, and many computer artists have utilized this process to great effect. But in principle the random process can be used in the generation of the program itself; a metarandom organization of the generative process. In practice this is likely to lead to many programs which are inexecutable on a given computer system, but an analogous process operates in human creativity. Many false starts and abortive attempts may be made before a workable design is produced.

This brings us to a new definition of computer art—art produced by the computer which is essentially out of the control of its operator. The entirely unexpected results of concatenations of program elements, intended to serve other mundane purposes. One of the finest graph plots I have come across was generated by an automatic drafting machine which inexplicably developed a fault and went on to produce a string figure of unusual beauty. Rerunning the program failed to reproduce the fault, which was an evanescent excursion into the realm of autogenic computer art.

Another example of computer generation is the Kaleidoscope program by DEC, which uses random inputs by the observer to build up the program controlling a dynamic display. Rather than the display being controlled by the user, the program is accreted under user initiation to produce a unique organization on each run. When this kind of activity is produced with sufficient flexibility, it can truly be called computer art.

The present inspiration for my work comes from the sinusoid—that mathematical wiggle which can transcend the operations of addition, subtraction, multiplication, division, integration and differentiation, and emerge unscathed. It is mathematically the simplest form of oscillation, and as such represents the whole domain of periodic events that mean so much in the process of life. The waves, the tides, the diurnal and seasonal variations. Light waves, sound waves, radiations and vibrations. Rotation and periodic cycles, repetitions and echoes, oscillations and pulsations, palpitations and ululations— all flow into the image I wish to produce.

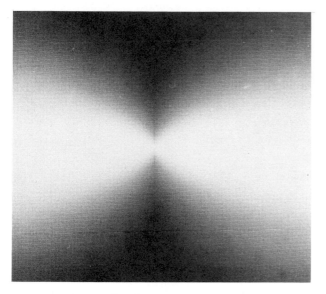

'Morphonome XXV'.

'Autonome III'.

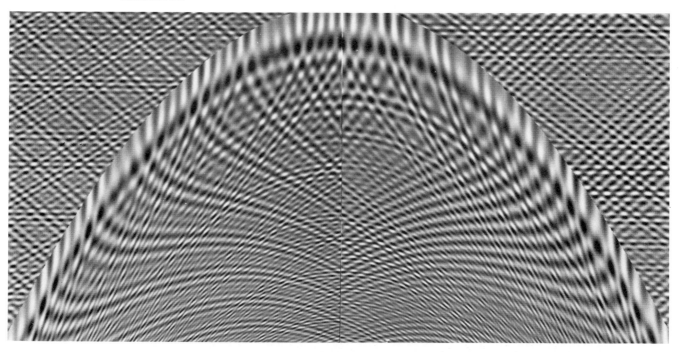

'Morphonome XI'.

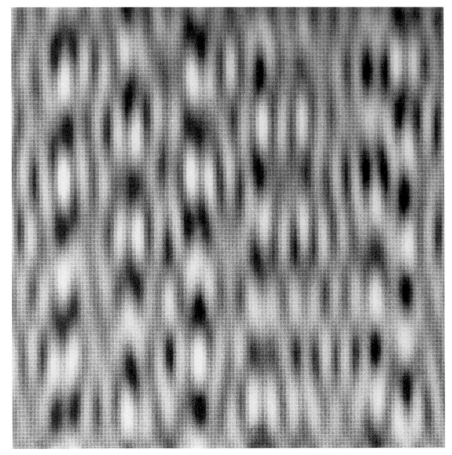

'Morphonome XII'.

In the study of human visual perception this mathematical tool has recently been introduced in the form of the sinusoidal (or blurred) grating. It is particularly useful for investigating the basis of visual responses to the environment because of its repetitive or multiple nature, which mirrors the repetitive or parallel organization of the neural pathways. This means that sinusoidal gratings are especially potent in producing visual illusions and distortions, because they can swamp the whole retina with the same kind of stimulation. Gazing steadily at images made up of these gratings will produce fluctuating, shifting impressions due to adaptation at several levels of the visual system. The very regularity of the pattern is the cause of its shimmering vitality in the brain of the perceiver.

I am particularly interested at this stage in avoiding the hard-edge, line-dominated form that typifies computer art at present. The microfilm plotter, which I have used mainly, allows continuous gradations in grey-level and opens wide possibilities for detailed control of the resulting image. In the Morphonome series I controlled the form of the image by a specific equation (hence the name) usually with a clear image in mind. But the Autonome series was produced with many functions under (random) control by the computer. I subsequently selected results that appealed to the human nervous system. The work represented here was all produced at Northeastern University on a CDC 6600 with a Calcomp plotter, or at Bell Laboratories on a Honeywell 6000 and a microfilm plotter.

San Francisco, California
September 1975

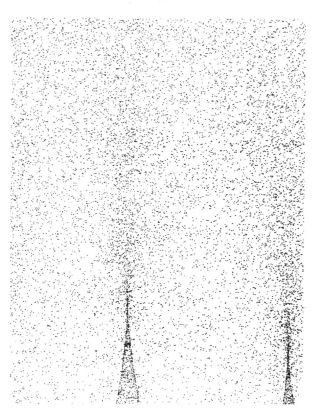

'Chaonome X'.

'Autonome X'.

MANFRED MOHR

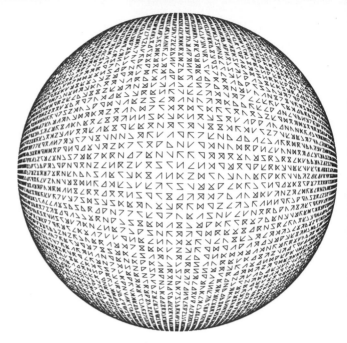

'Sphereless', 50 x 50 centimeters.

The fundamental view that machines should not be considered as a challenge to humanity but, like McLuhan predicted, as an extension of ourselves is the basic philosophy when becoming involved with technology.

A technology which 'functions' has to be integrated in our lives like a physical extension—a necessity of our body and our mind. We are living now in an era of enormous technological transitions, where so many misunderstandings in human machine relationships are created by lack of knowledge and the categorical refusal to learn by most individuals. A quasi mystical fear of an incomprehensible technology is still omnipresent.

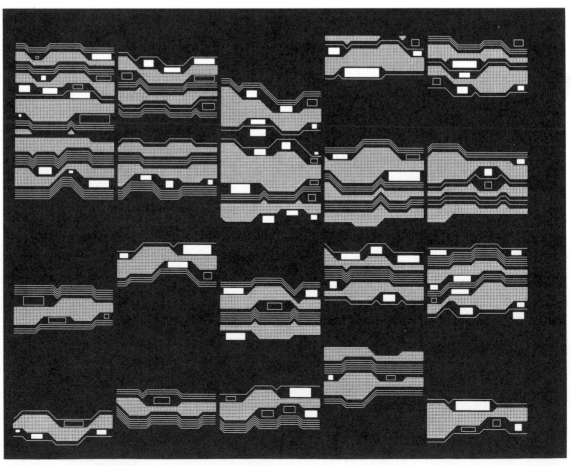

'Cluster Phobia', 51 x 51 centimeters.

'Combinatorial Framework of the Ordinal 15', 50 x 50 centimeters.

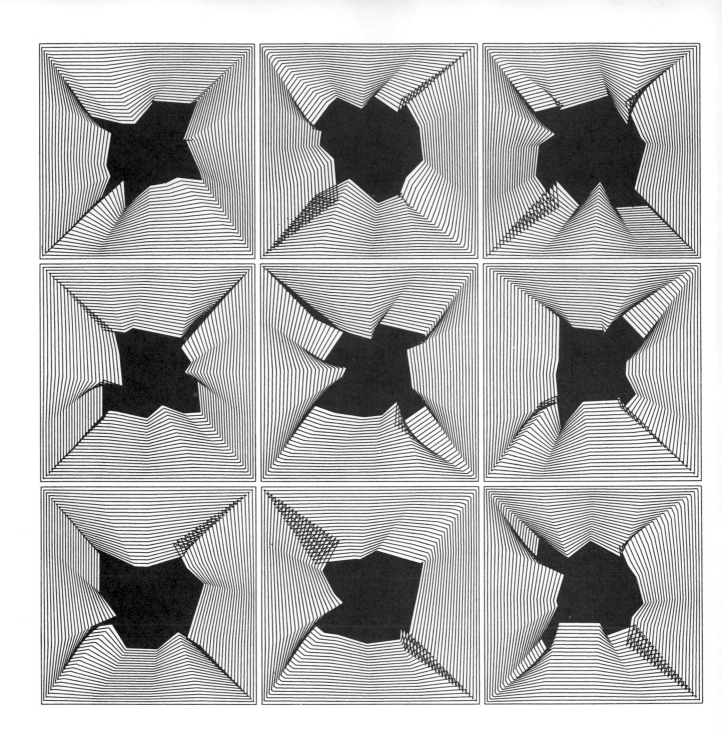

Breakthroughs in human development are always accompanied by radical changes of attitude towards the so-called human values. It is, for example, from a practical (and philosophical) point of view evident that one should simply be ready to leave the most possible part of a work to a machine when it becomes clear that in this way the desired solution may be better and more reliably achieved. It is also true that human thought can be 'amplified' by machines, raising our consciousness to a higher level of comprehension.

To apply methods of this kind in science is obvious, and generally considered as basic. To use similar methods in aesthetical research is, in my opinion, a possible and nevertheless historical consequence. Aesthetical research runs, for this point at least, parallel to scientific research and together they make our human developments more comprehensible.

In this context I consider the computer as a legitimate amplifier for our intellectual and visual experiences.

Through detailed programming analysis, one is able to visualize logical and abstract models of human thinking, which lead deep into the understanding of creative processing. Creative processes are mental processes having a priori an associative character, where associations are defined as interactions and/or transversal connections (Querverbindungen) of thoughts in a Time-Space neighbourhood relationship. Unifying those divergent or intersecting data from memory in order to form new meanings is called imagination or the facility of creating free associations. Most adults have been taught to think in a way which does not allow them to play with free associations. This 'cliche' thinking of so many people is radically opposed to imaginative thinking. To create new and perhaps important aesthetical information, it is

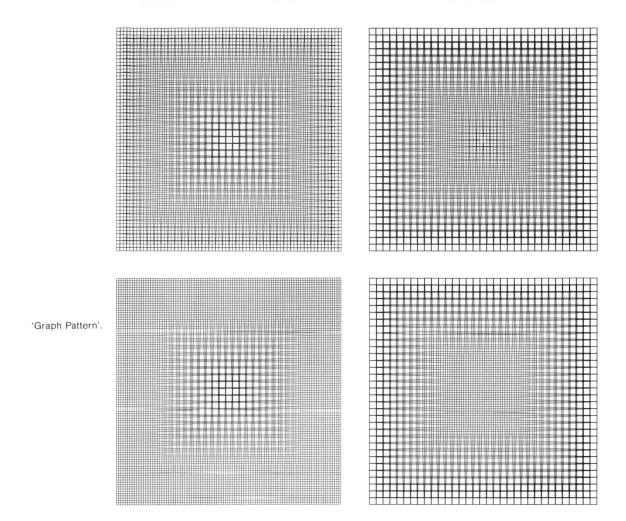

'Graph Pattern'.

necessary to operate with free associations. This does not necessarily involve a talent, but a training which has to be practiced. A computer, however, is (at least until today) not able to process in an associative way, even though it is a self-supervising machine. The computer is not conscious of what it is doing and can only execute orders from outside: from us! That means: a computer itself cannot create or invent anything.

We do not have to ask: what can the computer do?, but reverse the question by asking ourselves: what do we want to do? and then consider whether the help of a machine could be useful for our purpose. If the answer is positive, we have to find ways of asking the machine the right questions in order to get reasonable results, amplifying our thoughts and intentions. Proceeding in this way is an important step towards a systematic approach of aesthetical problems. Abraham Moles once said: "La machine ne pense pas, elle nous fait penser."

There are several ways of approaching the computer for this purpose:

1. A visual-concrete procedure. An existing visual image is dissected into its basic elements. Each element can represent an algorithm. One can operate in various ways with these elements. The experience is: visual image → process → visual image.

2. A statistical-flexible procedure. An existing or invented abstract logic is the basic algorithm and no visual image, or only a vague one, can be predicted. The importance of this approach lies in the applied rules, which are, at least in their conception, a new way of approaching a visual experience. The experience is: abstract logic → visual image.

Statistical-flexible procedures deviate into two distinct directions:

a) The visualisation of mathematical formulas. Without doubt very interesting results can appear which have never been seen before. For long-term artistic interest however, the resulting aesthetical information of a mathematical formula is in itself limited and therefore a closed system.

b) The research to find or invent individual rules as a means of artistic expression.

The individual impact of human behaviour, filtered and reformed through the inherent peculiarities of a computer, will lead directly to an interesting and overall coherent open system. Of course mathematics are used, but in this case only as a technical help, and not as the sole purpose.

The logical construction of a programming language forces us, on the one hand, to concentrate with an almost maniacal precision of formulation (the instructions), but opens, on the other hand, new dimensions for a wider and statistical thinking.

New operation models appear:
—Precision as part of aesthetical expression.
—High speed of execution and therefore multiplicity and comparativity of the works.
—The fact that hundreds of imposed orders and statistical considerations can be easily carried out by a computer instead of by the human mind, which is incapable of retaining them over a period of time, for example during plotting time (calculation time).
—The continuous feedback during a man-machine dialogue involves a learning process on the side of the

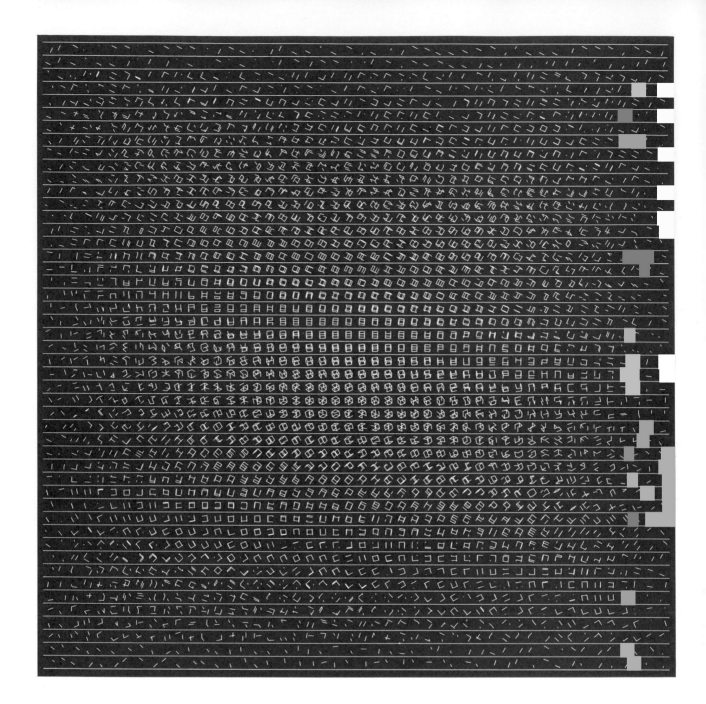

human being, resulting in a clearer image of the creator's thinking and intentions.

Properties of this kind form a conceptual basis that shows a rigorous attitude in dealing with aesthetical problems.

The dialogue with the computer implies also that results (graphics, etc.) and their visual expression have to be judged under completely new aspects. It is evident that one should not create single forms and judge them by a traditional and subjective aesthetic, but build sets of form where the basic parameters are relationships between forms with no aesthetical value associated to any particular form in the set. It is possible within this context to ignore the former 'good' and 'bad,' now allowing aesthetical decisions to be based on statistical and 'wertfreie' procedures, where the totality represents a quality of a quantity.

This procedure may lead to different and perhaps more interesting answers, lying of course outside one's normal behaviour but not outside the imposed logic. The above postulated conception becomes part of a conditioned aesthetical information.

Computer-aided art is too young a phenomenon for one to foresee all its influence on the arts. It is most probable that the importance of an art thus created might lie essentially in its subtle and rational way of proceeding, which means that not only the 'what' but also the 'how' of the change will have fundamental consequences for the future.

The world will not be changed from the outside but from the inside and aesthetical decisions will be more and more based on knowledge rather than on irrelevance. The shift from uncontrollable metaphysics to a systematic and logical constructivism may well be the sign of tomorrow.

Paris, France
February 1975

RUTH LEAVITT

I have been using the computer to make pictures for most of my career as an artist. When anyone asks me how I became involved with computers my retort is, "I married into it." My husband, Jay, teaches in the Computer Science Department at the University of Minnesota. Most of what I have learned has been through osmosis.

As a grand student of Hans Hofmann having studied painting with Peter Busa it seems strange, even to me, to be involved with anything mechanical. My art studies were firmly grounded in abstract expressionism—dripping paint, house paintbrushes, and the attitude 'I know nothing.' It is quite a leap to a computer, a plotter, and conscious decision making. However, the change has been gradual and I feel I am combining both attitudes, abstract expressionism and constructivism in my work.

My first encounter with computers in producing art was to experiment and create graphics with a program that already existed. I drew and shaded pictures on a cathode ray tube using a light pen attachment. The program had features which made it superior to drawing by hand. But after 6 months I was frustrated with it. Everything I drew so freely on the scope was ultimately resolved into a grid. This dissatisfaction, coupled with the fact that I now knew more about how computers worked, led me to think of my own idea for a program. I had had a rubber dollar bill when I was a child. I loved to stretch and distort the image on it.

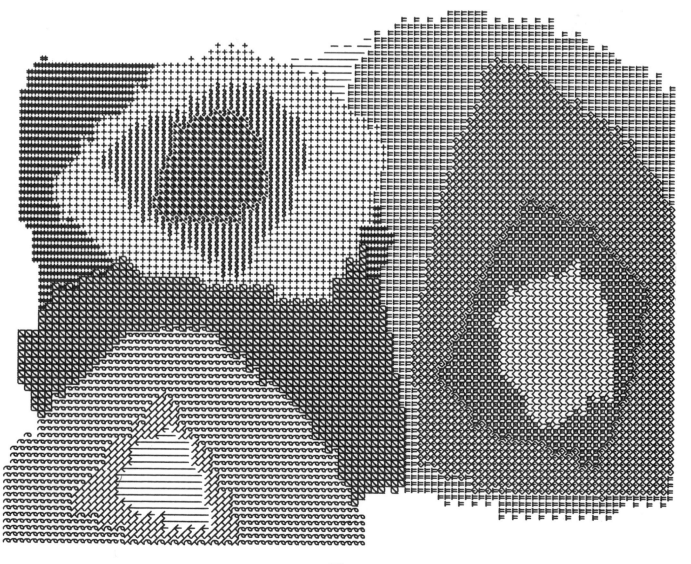

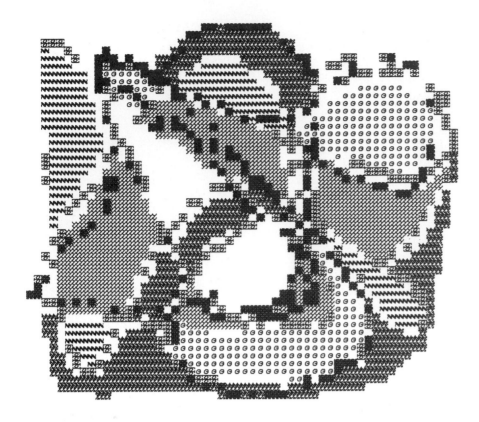

'Herringbone Variation III', serigraph.

My idea was to use the computer to simulate a rubber sheet and to stretch any patterns I wished to draw. Initially my patterns would be hard-edge, constructivist in style. But after distortion they would have the lyrical quality of abstract expressionism imparted to them. I have explored several patterns with this program, a linear one, one dealing with mass, a 3-dimensional projected figure, etc. Each series is unique, comprises a new style, and even requires its own method of stretching. I have used this 'stretching' program to create graphics and paintings. I am about to begin to use a variation of the program which incorporates transformations to make film animations. In addition, having conceived of one idea, I find myself bombarded with others. Recently, for example, I modified my stretch program to incorporate the idea of attraction and repulsion.

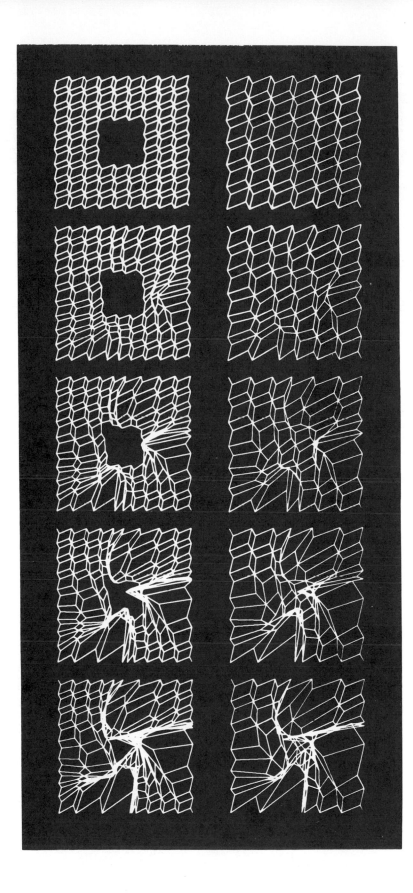
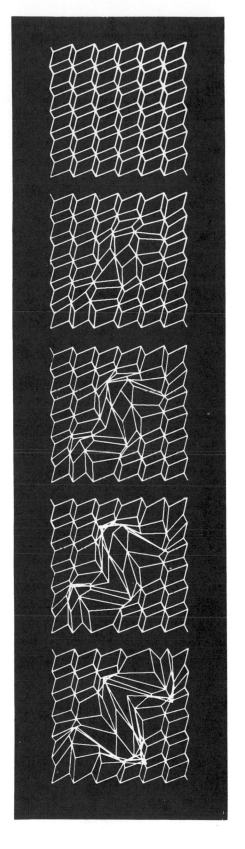

'Diamond Transformations I', serigraph.

'Prismatic Variation II', serigraph.

'Prismatic Variation V', serigraph.

'Inner City Variation II', serigraph.

I find that using the computer I do not have to give up my traditional role as artist. The machine acts as a multi-faceted tool which I control. When I began to use the computer I had no knowledge of programming. I have since taken a course on Fortran. This gave me an understanding of how the machine processes information, thereby giving me more control over my work. I do not actually code my programs, but I know what I can ask for and how to ask for it.

It is the option to create one's own work tools which, in my mind, makes computer art unique. A new role is now open to the artist in addition to the traditional one of making objects. He can create programs for himself, other artists, and perhaps even for the public. The impact of computers on art in the future will be greater because more artists will have access to machines. I have no doubt

that the public shall also have access to computers and certainly more leisure time. If computer art is to become 'the public art' it will not be because graphics can be produced cheaply and en masse as some have predicted. It will be 'the public art' because the public will be generating works of art with programs that artists have created.

As long as I have access to a computer, I will continue to use it. The machine allows me to create artworks that would probably be impossible to produce in any other reasonable way. With the aid of the computer I can now explore areas which artists in the past only thought possible to dream about.

Minneapolis, Minnesota
February 1976

KURT F. LAUCKNER

MICROPROCESSORS AND INTELLIGENT SCULPTURE

exhibit 'reflected intelligence' and those with 'internal intelligence.' The reflectively intelligent system accepts intelligent inputs to that sculpture, such as movement, temperature, light shadows, and sound, then it 'reflects' them back to the viewer in the form of sound, movement, etc. This type of sculpture does not make sophisticated decisions. The internally intelligent system, as one might guess, does indeed make intelligent decisions and 'thinks,' whatever that means! In the latter category, the microprocessor would probably be used as a controller of the sculpture and an interface to a larger computer. This is due to the magnitude of programs needed to do 'intelligent manipulations.' Figure 1 summarizes the two types of sculpture.

To better understand this division, it is helpful to examine a 'non-computerized' hypothetical sculpture. In the reflective case, Figure 2 shows the sculpture (a piano) with a keyboard input and sound output. The pianist's intelligent input is mechanically converted to sound and reflected back to him. An analogous intelligent sculpture could consist of a pianist, who hears the input sound from the viewer's piano and intelligently responds by playing the piano in a type of musical answer. The important feature in the latter case is that the pianist, who is part of the sculpture, is making intelligent decisions in responding to the viewer's sounds.

IS 100/B (Intelligent Sculpture, 100 Series/BIRDS)

I am currently designing two sculptures which fit the categories mentioned above. In particular, the BIRDS piece (a tentative representation is shown in Figure 3) exhibits reflected intelligence. It consists of several 'birds' which can move either up or down the pole (tree). As people observing the birds move around, movement sensors (ultrasonic-doppler shift sensors, commonly used as burglar alarms) cause the birds closest to the 'disturbance' to ascend their tree. If the movement persists after the bird reaches the top, then a rather unpleasant sound is emitted. The sculpture will force people to move slowly with caution, otherwise the disturbed birds cause unpleasant consequences. The coordination and control of the 'flock' of birds will be accomplished with a microprocessor.

Introduction With the inexpensive control capabilities now available via microprocessors and microcomputers, it is feasible to construct general purpose process control systems. These systems can be programmed to control a multitude of different sculptures without a tremendous investment in customized electronics. As more artists become aware of the capabilities and relative simplicity of these microcomputer systems, a new direction in artistic creation will evolve. It should be pointed out that several artists[1] have already worked in this direction.[2]

When examining this new creative area, it will be convenient to categorize the artistic works as to their sophistication, or better yet, their 'intelligence.' Two major categories immediately evident are works which

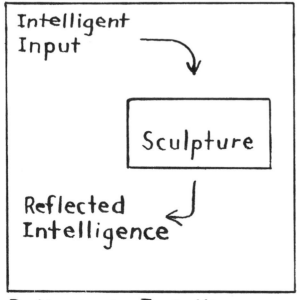

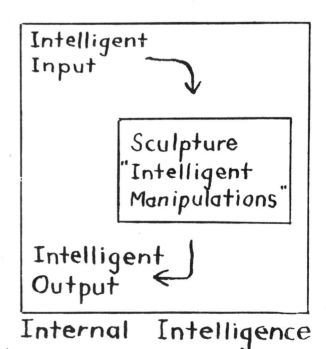

Figure 1

102

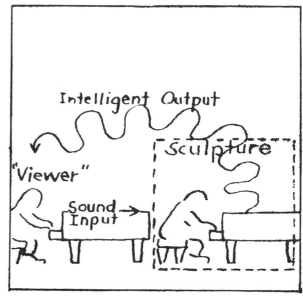

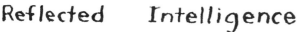

Figure 2

IS 400/D (Intelligent Sculpture, 400 Series/DECOY)

The second sculpture being designed is more complex. The hardware portion will consist of a 'decoy' sculpture placed in a large room as shown from overhead in Figure 4. Each viewer entering the room will wear a specially designed 'communications' helmet, which contains two independent communications systems. One system consists of an infrared transmitter and sensor. As a person looks about the room, the transmitter's signal is picked up by the sensors of the other helmets and additional fixed sensors placed in the room. A record of the individual's time and direction of observation is made for analysis by the computer. The second communications system is a low power radio transmitter which broadcasts information from the computer to each individual independently. This completes a 'closed loop' as shown in Figure 5.

The information broadcast to each viewer is in the form of synthesized speech. To better understand the content of the message, it is helpful to make a comparison with the conversational program PARRY developed by Colby, Weber and Hilf, 1971, as described by Jackson.[3]

PARRY is a program designed to simulate the conversational behavior of a paranoid human being. The conversation below was produced with the program operating in its 'weak version' of paranoia. Sentences labeled 'I' are produced by the human interviewer; those labeled 'O' by the program.

I —How long have you been in the hospital?
O—About a week.
I —Are you depressed?
O—No.
I —Were you taking drugs?
O—No.
I —What is your problem?
O—People make me nervous.
I —How do they do that?
O—They stare at me.
I —Why?
O—Maybe they don't like the way I look or something.
I —Do you look unusual in some way?
O—Why are you interested in my looks?
I —Because you said people stare at you.
O—Well, sometimes.
I —How do you get along with people?
O—I don't communicate very much with the others.
I —Why not?
O—They don't realize what's going on most of the time.
I —What is going on?
O—Do you know how the underworld operates?

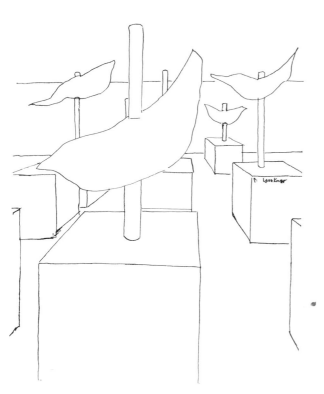

Figure 3

103

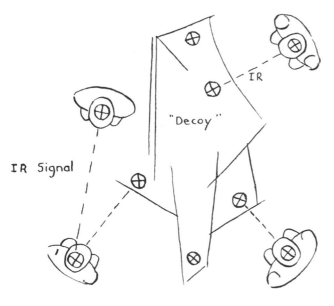

IR Signal

"Decoy"

IR

⊕ Infra Red Sensor

Figure 4

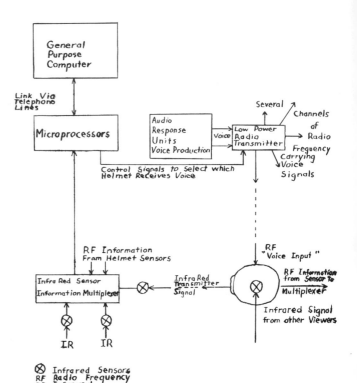

Figure 5

In the DECOY the input is in the form of the viewer's 'history of observation' coupled with additional information given to the sculpture's computer by a human assistant stationed within the room. This additional information would consist of various descriptors such as color of clothing, sex, physical features, helmet number, etc. The system will use this information to create various situations within the room. For example, what would you think, if suddenly everyone in the room looked at you? The reason for their stares could be the system's comment to everyone, that is, except you: "Look at that interesting cane the gentleman in the tan coat is holding." The people, their actions, and reactions are the sculpture, the physical sculpture in the room is only a decoy.

It is obvious to those working in artificial intelligence that the real problems with the construction of the sculpture are in the computer programs which make decisions about what to say to whom. The communication system, computer synthesized audio response, and other hardware features are relatively easy to construct. Of course, a large computer would be needed to do most of the analysis of information and formation of the audio response, but microprocessors would certainly be used for control purposes and as an interface to the large system. Depending on the complexity of the analysis and response programs, this could indeed be an intelligent sculpture.

Ypsilanti, Michigan
October 1975

FOOTNOTES

1. The Senster, 1971, by Edward Ihnatowicz, installed at the 'Evoluon' in Eindhoven, Netherlands. (See *Science and Technology in Art Today*, by Jonathan Benthall, p. 78.)
2. O.C.L.E.S. (Observer Controlled Light Emission System), 1974, by William Uphoff (see page 35, newsletter of the Computer Arts Society).
3. Jackson, Philip C., *Introduction to Artificial Intelligence*, Petrocelli Books, New York, 1974, p. 323.

VICKY CHAET

I learned to recreate geometric elegance, a nice gift for an artist. Learning it via computer was an art experience I want to discuss.

I would rather be showing video tapes of the computer generated geometrical images that turned me on, but the printed page is my opportunity for discussing my work. So here I am, a visual artist, giving forth words.

By the graces of the Industrial Engineering Department at Stanford University, I performed on the AGT 30 computer (Adage) geometric forms in three dimensionally illusioned space: glowing phosphors of the CRT display delineate a deep dark space. I interact with these TV images through analog controls.

The following is an account of my computer art experience.

"How did you become involved with the computer in producing art?"

I was sculpting in 1969. My boyfriend was reading Suzanne Langer's *Symbolic Logic*. I read it and felt that I needed logic to organize my approach to making art.

At the University of Massachusetts in 1969, my sculpture teacher, Robert Mallary, was already into the logic of computer art; and my landlord, Robert Archer, was a Computer Science professor. We had access to some sophisticated computer graphics displays at M.I.T. There I saw some graphics that graduate students had created in the wee hours of the morning. They were tired of working on an engineering problem and wanted to create some fun. I considered what they showed me art; I don't know what they called it. By 1971 I stopped sculpting and went to Stanford University to learn about computers. The Art Department at Stanford supported my computer interest for a couple of years before the Industrial Engineering Department took me in.

"What is your art background?"

Degrees: one Bachelor of Fine Arts degree; and two Masters of Fine Arts degrees, one in ceramics and one in sculpture. Shows: from 1963 to the present I have shown my work in ceramics, sculpture, computer-video, and painting in New York, Chicago, San Francisco, and Palo Alto.

In addition, I want to acknowledge in my background the French Impressionist paintings at the Chicago Art Institute which taught me everything about color. Even though my computer work is all black and white, my conception is in color.

"What role does the computer play for you?"

I gave the computer the role of tool. A tool to translate three dimensions to two, and a tool to animate frames for the moving picture which I would never choose to animate if I had to do it by hand.

I used a GRAFX language program written by Bill Brastow, on the faculty of Stanford's Industrial Engineering Department. The program was based on specifications which we put together in some delightful discussions concerning what would be fun to put through the computer. I always felt very serious and business-like talking with this man whose wit and intelligence whizzed around at the spaces where the talk became too technical for me to handle. The shapes which were easy to create with our program could be moved in any dimension by analogue dials controlling the X-Y-Z vectors. It is a very lovely machine—too temperamental about whether it wants to work today or not—but when it works, it works nicely!

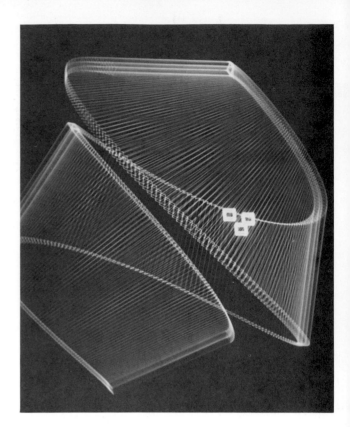

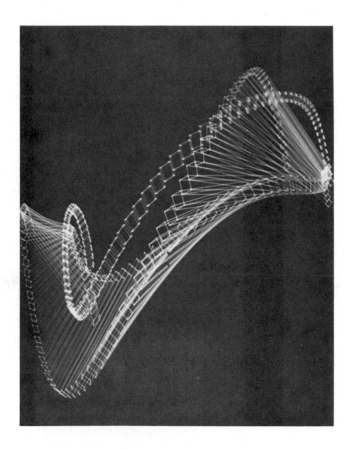

The program variables included position, shape, speed, scale and length. I could assign geometric paths to the moving forms with these variables. These variables could be independently assigned for each of the three positioning axes and for each object displayed. This meant that a subtle variety of paths was unanalyzable by a viewer. Yet the different factors between variables from one axis to one other was so small, and the final geometric shape simple and elegant, that it astounds the human mind which has no abstract number information. While the eye watches an illusion on two dimensional information, the mind perceives information as if it were three.

I put a human-like rhythm in the movements of the geometric shapes, so sometimes they seemed like excited anthropomorphic figures. I used video tape for my hard copy.

The computer was a tool for computation, drawing, animating, and displaying art forms.

"Are your computer works related to non-computer art?"

I feel it is related to the religious art of the old Middle East because of its pure geometry. In this century there is a lot of geometric art, take Moholy-Nagy as example of one artist.

"Do you have a final image in mind when work begins?"

A metamorphosis takes place between my ideas and the medium. I take into account the medium with its advantages and limitations. Eventually, working with a medium I am able to imagine the final material object when the work begins.

"Could your work be done without the aid of a computer?"

No. At least not by me. It would be tedious to animate.

"To what extent are you your own technician?"

I can load the program and run it. I have written and run a few simple programs (Stanford computer course homework for the most part). I cannot write programs for the images that I conceive of in my head.

"Do you intend to continue using the computer to create art pieces?"

Yes, when the machinery, technical artistry to compliment my traditional artistry, and financing, all come together.

"Where is your work seen?"

Only occasionally in special showings. It has been seen at Stanford University, DeAnza College, in the exhibition circuit at the Bloomfield Art Assoc. in Michigan and galleries in New York and San Francisco.

Palo Alto, California
October 1975

LILLIAN SCHWARTZ

"The art of any period is the result of the background factors of that age plus the personalities of its creative artists."—Bernard Myers .. Modern Art In The Making

I, Lillian Schwartz, (1927- ...) am a native of Cincinnati, Ohio and a graduate of the College of Nursing & Health of the University of Cincinnati.

I studied free-hand drawing at the University in 1948-1949, oil painting in St. Louis, Missouri, watercolors and woodcuts in Fukuoka, Japan and finally came to the New York area in the 50's and continued to study art.

An intense interest in new materials and its effects on continued stimulus to the creative process during the growth of a work of art led me to be aware of and to incorporate existing technology into my work.

I met and began working with Ken Knowlton, a computer scientist, in 1969, following the 'MACHINE' exhibition at the Museum of Modern Art. The international organization of Experiments in Art and Technology (E.A.T.) was founded "to try to establish a better working relationship among artists, engineers and industry."

In line with that purpose E.A.T. agreed to arrange a competition in connection with the 'MACHINE' exhibit. About 200 works were submitted. Of these, nine works were selected by Pontus Hulten, the director of the show, for inclusion in the exhibition.

My sculpture 'Proxima Centauri' and 'Studies in Perception 1,' a graphic, by Harmon and Knowlton were two of the exhibits.

The show catalogue describes 'Proxima Centauri' as, "Changing patterns appear on the surface of a white translucent dome, which at times seem to become a gelatinous mass that shakes, breathes, and then returns to still images. As the spectator approaches the sculpture, the dome throws off a red glow while slowly sinking into the base and thus inviting the viewer to come still closer to observe this phenomenon. The dome is now resting inside the base. Peering down into the rectangle, the viewer sees the spectacle of a series of abstract pictures focused on the globe ..."

The catalogue writes about 'Studies in Perception 1' ... "Computer graphics were created for utilitarian purposes. Among the uses are to study the field of view seen from the pilot's seat in an airplane, or to analyze a flat image in order to manipulate graphic data. The characteristics of the computer at the moment are strikingly shown in 'computer art.' The computer can act as an intelligent being: process information, obey intricate rules, manipulate symbols, and even learn by experience. But since it is not capable of initiating concepts, it cannot be truly creative; it has no access to imagination, intuition, and emotion." The last sentence can be applied to any medium but the previous sentence describes a medium that can process information, obey rules, and even learn by experience!

The awesomeness of such a tool places the artist in quite a humble position. There is a necessary kind of readjustment for the artist for here is a medium that may take some of the burdens from the artist. To find the real justification for the use of the computer by a painter would be to shift the emphasis by stimulating a new angle of approach; to maybe relieve the formal elements of some of the conscious emphases which are necessary and place more stress on content.

With such a medium we now have the means of displaying, in its constituent parts, images which possess simultaneously a number of dimensions.

To handle such a tool I find it necessary to break down these specific dimensions.

First, there are the more or less limited formal factors, such as line, tone value, and color. And, secondly, if the computer is used in filmmaking a knowledge of the craft of film.

As an example, when the artist considers line it is usually thought of as being a matter of simple properties such as length, angles, focal distance, and thickness. But measuring the characteristics of line by using a computer is of quite a different nature.

The associative properties once used by the non-computer artist no longer correspond to the direct will of the artist.

To perform the simple act of drawing a line over a page, exerting pressure on the pencil, charcoal or other instrument to change the thickness of the line or the direction becomes a major task in programming.

All rules concerning the use of the line must be well thought out in advance. With proper flexibility in a program one can accept or reject. The rewards eventually come when these lines can be positioned as desired. The artist can then contemplate the positions of these lines as drawn with any other medium but—with the computer an instruction can rotate the lines, join them, multiply them, or whatever instruction has been previously built into the program.

From this point, given mastery of the medium, the structure can be assured foundations of such strength that it is able to reach out into dimensions far removed from one's expectations.

It is no easy task for the artist to live with too much freedom in her medium. Great care must be given to the selectivity of these elements. Speaking from my own experience, it depends on my mood at the time of editing images into their final film form that decisions as to which of the many elements are brought out of their general order, out of their appointed array, and raised together to a new order and form. It seems clearer that the results of this medium may well fall into direct ascendancy of the hieratic

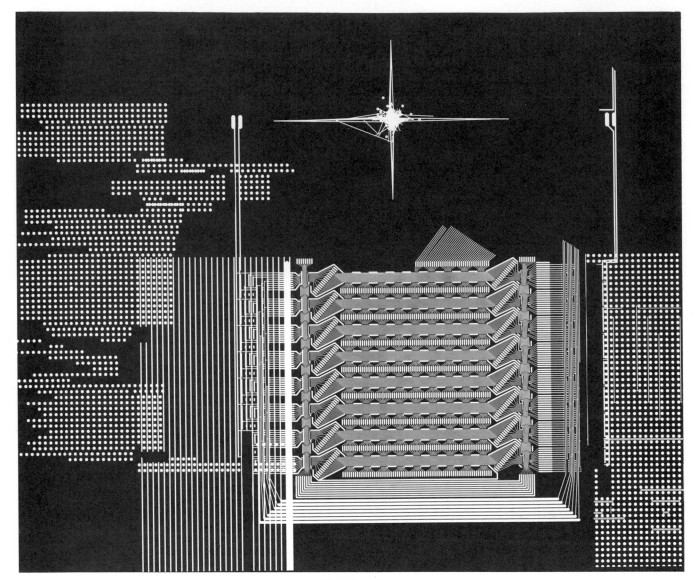

'Night Scene'.

forms of Seurat and the mosaics of Byzantium. The artists in India also worked from set Sudras. Even among the more recent artists Delacroix, Cezanne, and Matisse, the same desire for system and regularity for an ordered universe seem to dominate.

Artists must express their own creative character in the technology of their era in order to find their own historical and individual level.

The computer has also assisted me in the visualization of sculpture in three dimensions. Programs can be used to rotate sculptures, to view them stereoscopically, to place in a given site—all before any execution has taken place.

For the artist newly exposed to using the computer it is not unlike Stephen Leacock's hero, who jumped to his horse and dashed madly off in all directions.

Watchung, New Jersey
November 1975

LARRY ELIN

SYNTHAVISION: SERENDIPITY FROM THE NUCLEAR AGE

It is not at all an unusual phenomenon that, in the course of scientific inquiry, one discovery begets another and subsequent breakthroughs produce an unintended chain of pleasant surprises. So it was that physicists studying the effects of radiation on domestic and military structures developed an exciting and unique method for producing computer generated animation.

The new animation technique is called Synthavision and is marketed commercially by Computer Visuals, Inc., of Elmsford, New York. Using the process, dimensional, shaded objects can be made to perform a countless variety of complicated movements and captured on film. Amazingly, the objects don't have to exist. The need for art work, photographs or prototypes has also been eliminated, since Synthavision enables the animator to produce his 'actors' within the software of the computer *mathematically*.

This incredible attribute is an offshoot from the work which inspired the development of Synthavision in the first place. Scientists at Mathematical Applications Group, Inc., Computer Visuals parent company, were conducting experiments in which whole environments were mathematically described to a computer (an IBM 360/65). These mathematical models were then 'exposed' to a hypothetical dose of radiation. The program then in use diagnosed the effects of the radiation on the objects in the environment—how much reflected off, defracted within or penetrated. Although neither the environment nor the radiation existed, the findings were accurate and applicable to real life.

Because radiation and light rays have many of the same characteristics, the scientists, led by Dr. Phillip Mittelman and Robert Goldstein, theorized that mock situations such

This chess set shows some of the fine detail that can be managed using simple geometric shapes to construct more complex ones.

The engineers and designers at the Boeing Company supplied all the specifications necessary to make a film of this Heavy Lift Helicopter before it was ever built.

as these could be programmed exposing the objects to light rays instead of radiation. All of the light would, of course, reflect off the solid objects in the program. The program could include a command to direct the reflected light to a single point which would act as an 'eye,' or camera. The light reflected off the objects and to the camera would create an image of the objects. Years of research followed, and the result is Synthavision, complete with mathematically described objects, camera and light source—all of the elements necessary to create a film studio situation in the memory of the computer.

The input for this child of the nuclear age includes descriptions of the objects, or 'actors' in the film, the location and characteristics of a camera (focal length and size of image plane), the direction from which the light is coming and a set of instructions called 'Director's Language,' which tell the computer how to treat the objects (animate the actors) in the film.

These variables are first determined by the animator, and then key punched in a specified, very easy to use, format designed expressly for Synthavision. Based on the information, the IBM 360/65 computer makes extensive calculations to determine what the object looks like in each frame of the movie. It outputs, in digital form, the frame by frame mathematical descriptions of the objects on magnetic tape. The tape is then mounted on a mini-computer, whose function is to read the tape and output the information piecemeal—one frame at a time. The electronics of a graphics display machine converts the digital information to analog form. This signal is then displayed on a Cathode Ray Tube (CRT), from which it is

photographed by conventional animation cameras. It may sound like a long, drawn out process, but it is really quite fast, although by no means real time. A computer animator could produce a one minute film in about 1/3 the time required of a hand animator.

"How," you may ask, "does one describe an object to the computer?"

It is really quite simple. Synthavision incorporates a technique known as combinatorial geometry, whereby whole, voluminous shapes such as boxes, spheres and cones are added or subtracted to form more complex shapes. The equations for these shapes, and others, have already been programmed into the computer's memory. The animator need only call for them, designate their location and size and inform the computer which shapes are solid and which are to be invisible—a trait necessary to subtract one volume from another. Almost any known or imagined object can be described to the computer this way. The animator 'models' his objects in much the same way as a sculptor might use old pipes and scraps of wood to create a work of art. The animator using Synthavision has more flexibility, however, because he can cause his object to move and, in a sense, come to life.

Movement is given to the actors by key punching commands to move, turn or scale the objects in a certain number of frames. The camera can also be made to move or rotate. A typical command might be to move the object in 120 frames (five seconds) from point A to point B, while simultaneously rotating the object about point C. The computer calculates what the object looks like in each of those frames and writes the information on magnetic tape.

When the frames are viewed sequentially, the illusion of movement has been created.

If there is one very obvious advantage of the Synthavision process, it is the scientifically accurate shading and perspective maintained by the objects regardless of how they are moved or turned. They appear to be real, though somehow cartoonish in nature. Indeed they should since, as far as the computer is concerned, they *are* real. The effect of reality is created in the software by assigning a gray level to the points on the surface of the described object. The gray level is determined by the orientation of the point with respect to the camera and the light source. The more acute the angle, the brighter that point will be. A sphere, for example, will be brightest where its exposure to the light source is most direct, and will gradually become darker as its surface curves away from direct exposure.

There are other very attractive attributes of Synthavision. It is very fast. An animator, in order to produce one minute of film, would have to *draw* 1440 cels or pictures, each a little different. There are short cuts which are commonly used to reduce this number to some extent, but the fact remains that one minute of film requires long hours at the drawing stand. Each drawing would then have to be inked (outlined) and opaqued (colored) and finally filmed. All of these steps are done manually, for the most part, and require a variety of skills and personnel. A computer animator need only to describe the picture elements once and then command the computer to produce the necessary pictures. The computer also 'opaques' and performs the filming. It accomplishes all of these tasks at great speed, freeing the animator for creative rather than manual endeavors.

The tremendous flexibility, expediency, and accuracy of Synthavision testifies to the potential for the computer in the animation and Graphic Arts fields. When you consider that Synthavision is actually in a very early stage of development, the future appears even more favorable—both for Synthavision (and whatever follows), and for Computer Graphics in general.

Elmsford, New York
October 1975

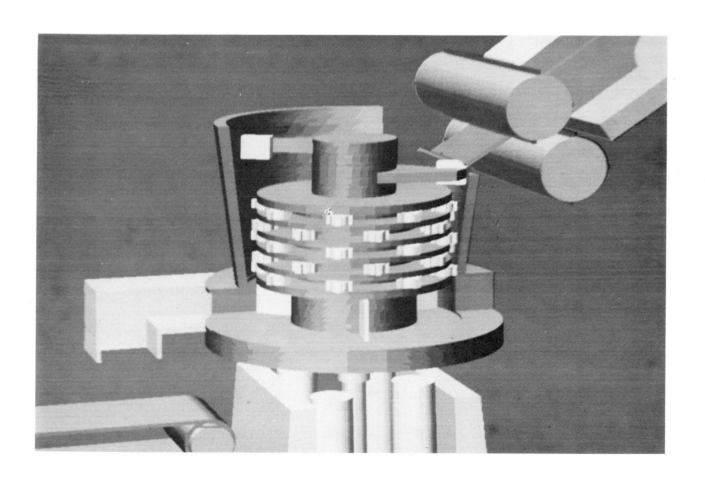

The function of this machine is to chew whole cars into pieces about the size of a quarter. Obviously the process cannot be photographed from the inside, but Synthavision showed in a representational fashion how it works.

HIROSHI KAWANO

WHAT IS COMPUTER ART?

Computer art is the art of computer as an artificial intelligence. A computer can solve an algorithmic problem by digital computing. Therefore, as long as art has an algorithmic procedure, a computer should be able to have its own artistic behavior. Although the aesthetic quality of art seems to have been overstressed in our modern art because of the philosophical influence of epistemological subjectivism since the 18th century, art properly has its generative base on the same human reason as in the case of science as shown in the classic Greek art and Renaissance art. This tells us that art is one kind of logical activity in its essence. Here is the raison d'etre of computer art.

A computer can produce its own works of art by representing the logic of artistic procedure which is hidden in human art. So this representing process is called the simulation of human art by computer. But the computer's ability to simulate art is given by a programmer who lets the computer produce works of art by teaching it the algorithmic procedure of art as a program. This relationship between programmer and computer can be paralleled with the one between parent and his child. A parent teaches his child how to draw a picture, for example, and tries to let him grow up to achieve it by himself. This 'how to draw' is the algorithmic procedure of picture-drawing. In order to do so, the parent must beforehand know the algorithm of picture-drawing which he is now trying to teach his child. The more explicitly he knows and can teach the algorithm, the better the drawn picture of his child will become; that is, the quality of the picture his child drew depends only upon the quality of the algorithm the parent had possessed already and taught his child. The role of a programmer in computer art seems to be similar with this parent's role.

Thus a computer artist should be a programmer who can teach his computer to produce works of art by itself, and furthermore know about the digital computing behavior of his computer in detail. It is never a computer artist, but a computer itself that produces works of art; a computer artist only helps his computer acting as a programmer. It looks as if God controlled a human artist as the creator who had programmed the activity of a human artist. In this meaning, the computer art should not be confused with a style or a school of the modern art using a computer as an innovative tool of an artist who has been tired of traditional techniques of art. As the latter usually seems to be called 'computer art,' I would like to call the former art of computer 'art computer.'

'Art computer' has an artificial creativity corresponding to the level of the program given by a programmer and behaves by the control of a program. This means only the logic of the structural procedure controls composing the required work from data after generating them automatically. It never means that the control results from the data themselves which are necessary to determine the sensuous surface of the finally completed work. Therefore, art computer has the programmed tendency of generating many possible compositions with various

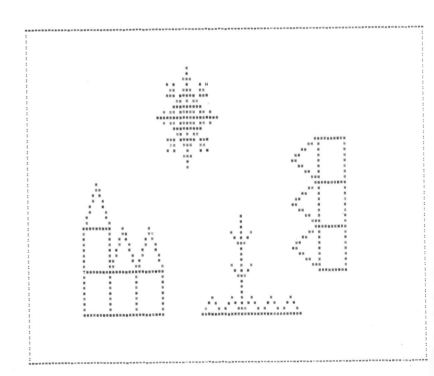

112

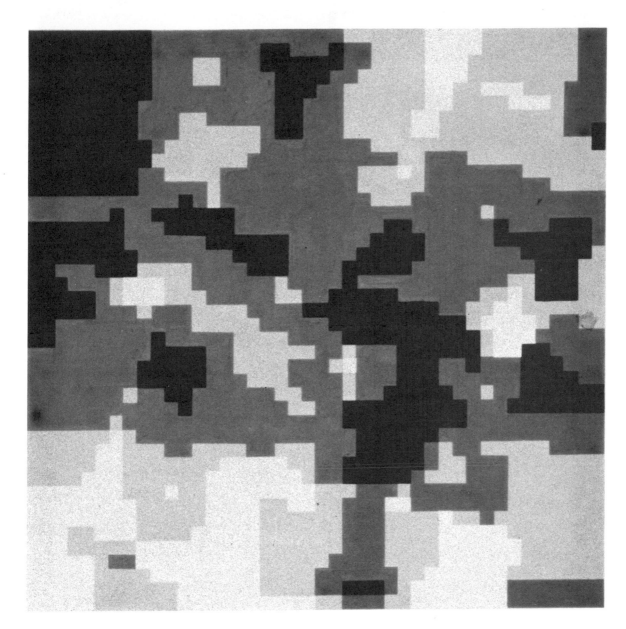

modifications in general, and the freedom of selecting an unique work among them according to the program and its input data. This large possibility of production and the variability of the final image an 'art computer' produces is surely the key of its artificial creativity.

As mentioned above, an 'art computer' cannot simulate a human art until the algorithm of art is found and described as a program. But this algorithm of art can be made clear only by scientific aesthetics. In this meaning, the work of 'art computer' is an experimental product of scientific aesthetics. Only the new scientific aesthetics which has replaced the old traditional aesthetics can provide an effective method of programming for 'art computer' because the algorithm, that is the digital computing logic of art, can be cleared up only by scientific aesthetics. Here is a favorable cooperation of art and science which can surely be found in the mature period of art history. Thus, the ability of 'art computer' to produce works with a high artistic quality depends on the degree of understanding of human art in scientific aesthetics. That is, the praxis of 'art computer' is connected tightly with the science of human art.

The computer artist as a programmer should not be a so-called artist who has a sense instead of a reason, but be a scientist of art with logical thinking for whom a rigorous stoicism against beauty is necessary. He may only program for his 'art computer,' and the 'art computer' will produce its works following the given program. In this meaning, just an art computer should be called artist, and a so-called computer artist is not an artist, but a teacher of an 'art computer.' Let's call the teacher of artist (= 'art computer') meta-artist, then it is this meta-artist that is truly needed for an 'art computer.'

Lastly, how can such an algorithmically produced work as mentioned above possess its aesthetic quality? This answer must be obtained from an 'art computer' itself! We cannot feel even another man's human feeling, much less computer's feeling! The works of 'art computer' would show such an aesthetic quality as beautiful, sentimental, comic etc. only for the appreciator with an empathy to it. However, this philosophical problem now doesn't seem so instructive for our 'art computer.'

Tokyo, Japan
September 1975

ROGER VILDER

My work is centered around a few physical and emotional feelings such as the growth of a shape or form, the filling of a crack, the expansion and contraction of matter, the change, mutation, metamorphosis of a shape. Coupled to those feelings are some more rational concerns such as the relationship of a unit to the whole, the similarities of motion cycles and evolution in different worlds seemingly without connections.

Most of these feelings and concerns are conveyed by my works: gears revolving all at the same time, with patterns of colour repeated on each gear surface, creating optical illusions and colour changes due to eye fatigue; square linear shapes out of steel coil, expanding and contracting in a given path; gel silicon cubes disintegrating into organic motion when vibrated; neon lines revolving and creating an electric light ballet; lines moving on a surface, constantly changing the proportions of the divided areas. All those works are made of mechanical components. They come alive only when in motion, since motion is the vehicle to express visual phenomena.

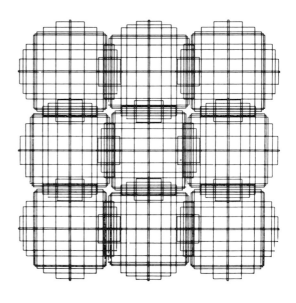

variation 1, 9 x 9 inches, 1973.

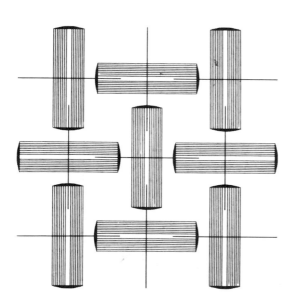

variation 6, 9 x 9 inches, 1973.

This statement was prepared originally to accompany a portfolio of computer art published by GALERIE + EDITIONS GILLES GHEERBRANT, Montreal, Canada.

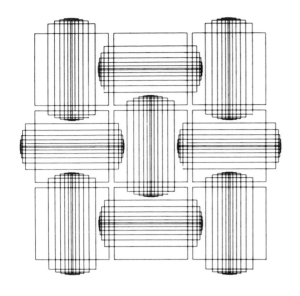
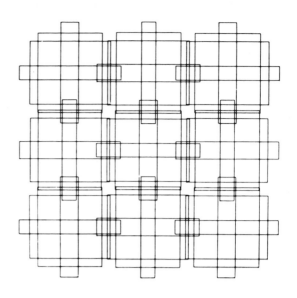
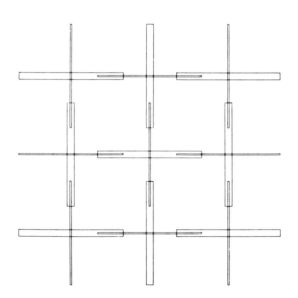
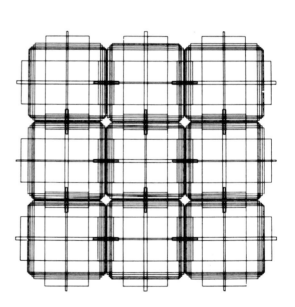

Variations from a film sequence.

When I began to work with computers, my first reflex was to recreate on the cathode-ray tube most of the visual phenomena I had created by mechanical means. Soon I realized the amazing potential of the computer and began to expand my ideas into more graphically oriented work. As a result, I produced some short animation films.

I found myself very much at ease with a computer, mainly because I was already used to working within a defined system, with the constraints of mechanics. Yet there is a great difference between computer art and other media. The exchange, while the process of creation is happening, seems more alive because of its instantaneity. It is almost like having a conversation with someone from which something visual results. This very aspect of the computer, along with its extraordinary speed of execution, is what I appreciate most when working through this medium.

Montreal, Canada
June 1974

JACQUES PALUMBO

In my present research I am trying to render communicable the substance of the content of the work of art on a perceptual and reflective level.

As a starting point, it was necessary to analyse the occidental thinking process which is essentially linear and consequently defines a principle of cumulative knowledge. In a second stage of my work (which I am presently pursuing) to concretize this type of thought I am seeking to create a form for the content of my research and to outline a reading by means of my work which is not only linear but multi-directional or 'tabular.'

In the first stage of my work, I constructed my research on numerical signs, alphabetical signs and signs of punctuation. It was necessary to build a system to give a 'verticality' to the typographical sign. Why typographical signs? Because these signs, already coded and codified, define the structure of the language and, consequently, of communications. These coded signs have an 'order' in space: my aim was to redefine this space. My tools (hardware) during this research period were a typewriter and paper; as for the software, it was a semiological analysis.

For my analysis I used the repertoire of numerical signs (87) and visual signs (10 picas) on my machine. Because these signs have a sequence, they can be declined. Consequently I placed this repertoire on a paradigmatic axis ... As in narrative prose, the descriptive enumeration successively articulates elements chosen at random and subsequently assembled in an arbitrary order. After the enumeration, the signs define a permutable order, then combine. On the syntagmatic axis going from left to right, I observe an evolution in which there is a transition from a serial order to a permutable order. I realized that the force of a sign depends not on its semantic value, but rather on its relationship to neighboring signs. To concretize this notion of semiotics, during the second stage of my research, I stripped the sign of its semantic value and gave it a purely spatial character. I thus replaced the substance of the content with a form of the content, reiterating Eco's theory which states that: "In order to be communicable, the substance of the content must be made into a 'form of the content' structurally homologous to its form of expression."

'0804197219H21'.

116

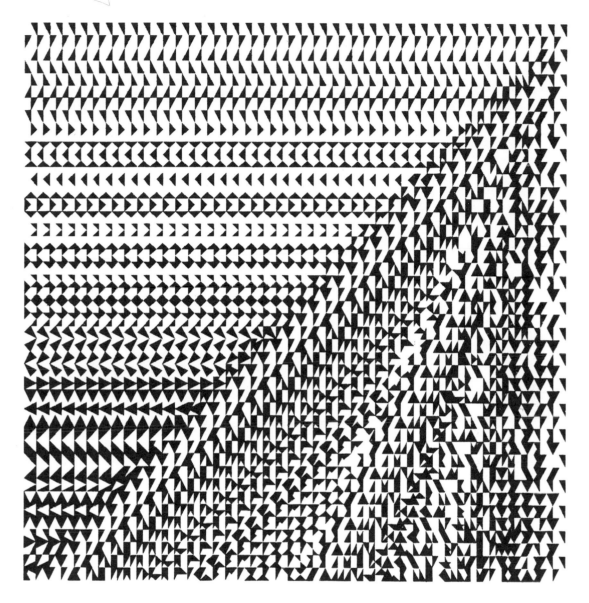

Electrostatic drawing, 1973.

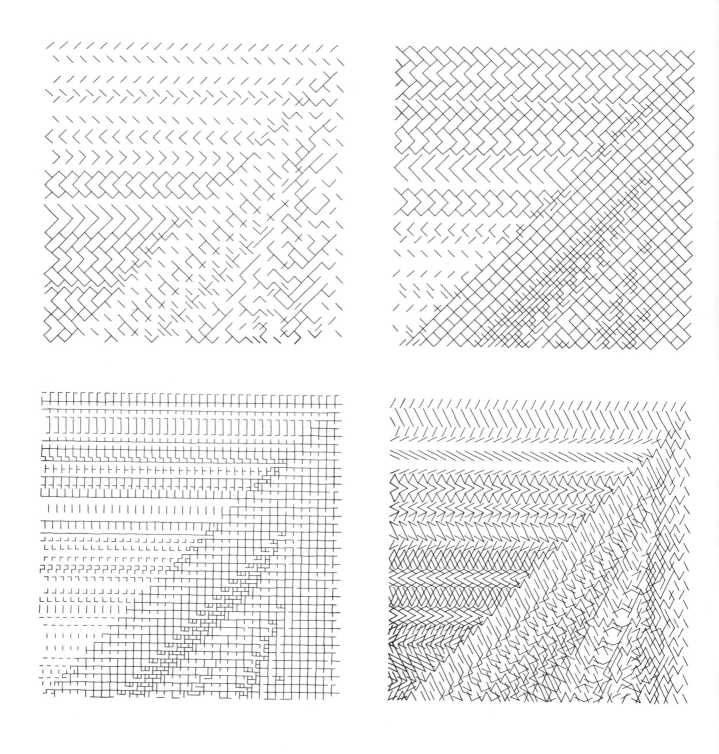

'SOF2B 12291 120573'   'SOF2A 12289 100573'
'SOF1C 12285 060573'   'SOF2C 12302 230573'

118

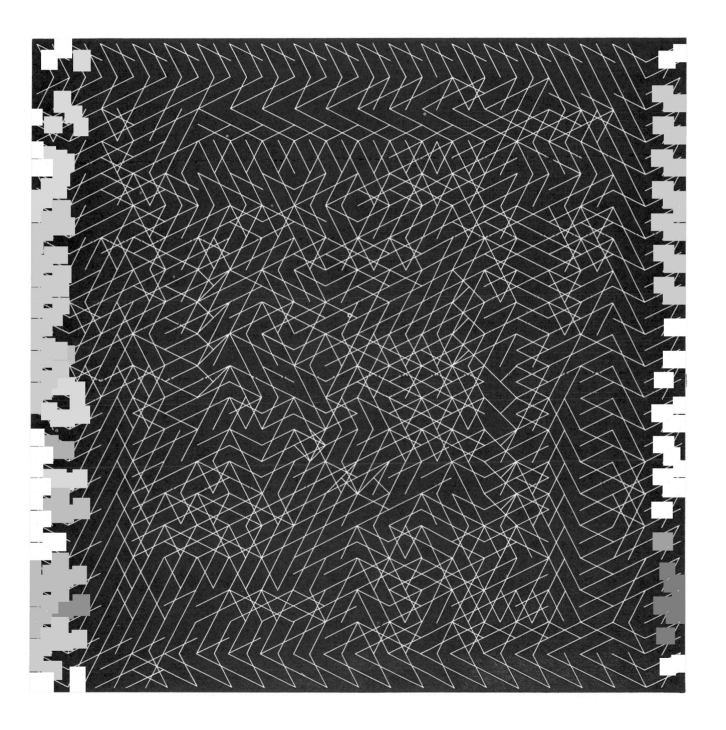

'HE7 gc/gf', 1974, 26 x 20 inches. Serigraph from the 'OPEN SIGNS'
portfolio.

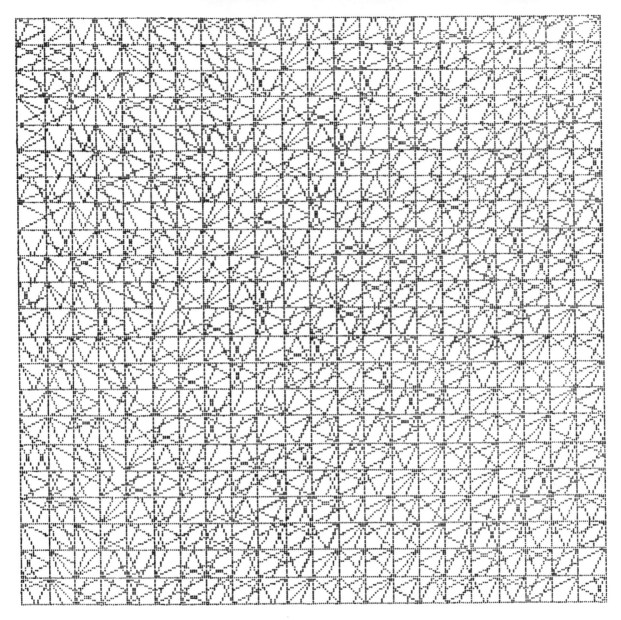

'HIJ gf/gc', 1973; serigraph, 26 x 20 inches.

In practical terms, for each typographical symbol, there is a corresponding graphic sign to which I have attributed a spatial value. An enumeration on a numerical base can be seen in each vertical column. Therefore, in each horizontal line, each sign has a value equivalent to that of the sign preceding and following it, but with a different numerical base:

1	1	1	1
2	2	2	10
3	3	10	11
4	10	11	100

4 (base 5) = 10 (base 4) = 11 (base 3) = 100 (base 2)

Technically speaking, my work was well suited to experiments with a computer. I worked in collaboration with the Centre de Calcul de l'Universite de Montreal. Several experiments done with an electrostatic points printer (Versatec) offered a new dimension to my work relating to the concept of time. The machine does not make errors and the visual experience is almost immediate since, having given the data to the computer, I received the result in 'real time.' The concept of sensitivity takes a new meaning. It corresponds to what I would call a new program which, instead of addressing the senses and intuition, speaks far more to the intellect and to the reason by means of a more and more subtle coding. During this stage I used the computer, not to test its capacities, but to discover the maximum of 'interesting' possibilities it had to offer.

I maintain that the work of art is a fundamentally ambiguous message: a plurality of 'signifiers' which exist in one single 'signifiant.' To make known that the world is an object which must be deciphered ... to transform signs, is to give them a new distribution in nature (this undertaking is indeed the definition of art) and to base this distribution not on 'natural laws,' but on the freedom that men have to give a meaning to things (cf: Brecht's theater).

The role of art is therefore not so much to know the world as to produce complements to it: art creates autonomous forms, which, added to those existant, possess a life of their own and laws unto themselves.

Montreal, Canada
August 1975